Poetry

Selected Poems
BY WITTER BYNNER

The Collected Poems
OF STEPHEN CRANE

The Collected Verse
OF ROBERT HILLYER

Slow Wall. Poems: New & Selected
BY LEONORA SPEYER

Collected Poems
OF ELINOR WYLIE

THESE ARE BORZOI BOOKS
PUBLISHED BY ALFRED A. KNOPF

❊ IN AMERICAN ❊

G MAILLARD KESSLERE. B.P.

IN
AMERICAN

THE COLLECTED POEMS OF

JOHN V. A. WEAVER

With a Foreword by

H. L. MENCKEN

NEW YORK   LONDON

ALFRED · A · KNOPF · 1939

Robert Clayton
.25
6-24-47
10-17-47

Copyright 1923, 1926, 1927, 1928, 1930, 1939 by
Alfred A. Knopf, Inc.

Copyright 1932 by John V. A. Weaver

All rights reserved. No part of this book may be reproduced in
any form without permission in writing from the publisher, except by a reviewer who may quote brief passages in a review to
be printed in a magazine or newspaper. Manufactured in the
United States of America.

FIRST EDITION

Published simultaneously in Canada by the Ryerson Press

THE FIRST TIME I can recall hearing of Johnny Weaver was in the early Spring of 1919, when he submitted a little satirical sketch in prose to the *Smart Set*. It was not more than three hundred words long, but he had separated it grandiosely into three chapters, marked off by Roman numerals. It went into type at once and the author received a very prompt check — probably for $5. The *Smart Set,* in those days, had little money in its till, but though we were thus forced to pay badly we took pride in paying almost instantly, and to the younger authors of the country that was something, if perhaps not much. Johnny, like the rest, was apparently delighted, and began sending in more of his compositions, some in prose and the rest in verse. The sketch aforesaid, "Afternoon Tea" by title, was printed in the issue for June, 1919. His first poetical contribution, a sonnet called "Emotion Bourgeoise," appeared a month later. The title here, I suspect, was an afterthought, added in confession and avoidance, for the sonnet itself was very sentimental stuff. Its thesis was that the scent of lilacs will often remind a young fellow of a lost sweetheart who patronized that flower, and that his memories of her, crowding upon him, will considerably upset him.

Johnny was then but lately out of the Army that had been raised to save democracy, and was enjoying a job on the

Chicago *Daily News* — not, as I remember, on the editorial staff, but in the business office. However, Henry Blackman Sell, who was literary editor of the paper, had no prejudice against the suspicious characters downstairs, and when Johnny applied for books to review he was accommodated. The legend is that Sell promised him a steady commission if he could write a review that would sell a designated number of copies of a designated book in a designated advertiser's store during a designated three days, and that Johnny accepted the challenge and achieved the feat. This may be either true or false, but the fact is established that the boy from downstairs was soon writing reviews every week, and hobnobbing with the literati who have always embellished the *News* office. The stars at that time were Carl Sandburg and Ben Hecht. Sandburg, with " Chicago Poems " four years behind him, was writing editorials, and Hecht, after a gaudy career in the city-room, was about to return from a brief tour of duty as correspondent in Germany. Soon afterward Sandburg was promoted to the job of movie critic, then something new in journalism, and Hecht began concocting the bitter sketches that afterward became " 1001 Afternoons in Chicago."

It was in the same Spring of 1919 that Alfred A. Knopf published the first edition of my book, " The American Language." Knopf and I were both so uncertain about it that it was brought out in a limited edition of 1500 copies, but it sold out almost at once, and I have been doing new editions of it ever since. That first edition closed with some rhetoric that soon succumbed to more interesting stuff, but

while it lasted it set Johnny to writing in the American language — the first poet, so far as I know, to attempt that opera-
tion, and the most successful to this day. Here is the passage:

> Given the poet, there may suddenly come a day when our
> *theirns* and *woulda hads* will take on the barbaric stateliness
> of the peasant locutions of old Maurya in " Riders to the Sea."
> They seem grotesque and absurd today because the folks who
> use them seem grotesque and absurd. But that is a too facile
> logic and under it is a false assumption. In all human beings,
> if only understanding be brought to the business, dignity will
> be found, and that dignity cannot fail to reveal itself, soon or
> late, in the words and phrases with which they make known
> their high hopes and aspirations and cry out against the intol-
> erable meaninglessness of life.

These lofty words were mistaken, by some of the critics of
the time, for irony, and they treated the whole book as an
exercise in humor, but Johnny out in Chicago took it seri-
ously, and was soon hard at work backing it up. The first
result was a set of free verse in forty-five lines, entitled " Élégie
Américaine." When it reached the *Smart Set* office, which
was early in the Summer of 1919, it fetched $11.25, and in
September of the same year it was duly embalmed in print.
I do not recall that it brought in any considerable flow of
felicitations from subscribers, but nevertheless it attracted the
attention of not a few practitioners of the then fashionable
art of free verse, and in a little while the office was flooded
with imitations of it. But Johnny had the right of way, and
we allowed him his monopoly. In the course of the ensuing

year he composed enough other pieces in American to make a book, and Knopf brought it out in January, 1921. It made a large and resounding success — in fact, it leaped far ahead of nearly all the other free verse that was roaring from the press at the time. There were seven printings by the end of the year, and before sales began to slacken there were thirteen editions altogether. Johnny followed it, in 1923, with "Finders," which ran to six editions; in 1925, with "More in American," which ran to two; and in 1928, with "To Youth," which also ran to two. In the last-named he began to ease away from the vulgate: some of the poems in it were in conventional forms, and employed the conventional materials of light verse. He was by then in Hollywood.

This hegira came after four years as literary editor of the Brooklyn *Eagle* — a dull job, and one that must have fretted him. I used to see him often at the Algonquin. The eminent literati who sat at its Round Table looked down their noses at him, for he was hardly one to show a due reverence for greatness, but I found him an amusing fellow, and we commonly palavered at length whenever we met in the lobby. He was then full of plans for novels, and a couple of them were eventually executed. But the critics were cold and the public failed to buy — at all events, in any passionate and satisfying way. His real interest, I suspect, was always in the theatre. He had gone to Harvard from Hamilton to sit under the celebrated George Pierce Baker, and one of his classmates there was Eugene O'Neill. Baker took a low view of his gifts, and is said, in fact, to have prophesied formally that he would never write a play. When, years later, he did "Love 'Em and

Leave 'Em" with George Abbott, and it made a success on Broadway, he delighted in recalling this injudicious prognostication. How much Johnny wrote of that play and how much Abbott wrote I don't know, but the title came from a poem printed in "Finders" in 1923. When, in 1930, he published "Turning Point," he dedicated the book to Abbott and five others who, "in one way or another, almost succeeded in keeping me from going insane in Hollywood during 1929."

His adventures there were full of the frustrations and disgusts that all other writers of any sense encounter. The movie moguls were never able to fathom so direct and candid, not to say tactless a man: they were used to much smoother and more politic fellows. At the start, Johnny found one understanding soul in King Vidor, the director, and together they put together "The Crowd," which still appears regularly in all the recurrent lists of the World's Best Movies; but after that there was a hiatus until the talkies began to come in. Johnny was sent for as an expert in the common speech, and fell upon his new duties with great enthusiasm. He prepared the script for "Tom Sawyer" and had a hand in various other excellent talking films. He liked the work, but in the end the malignant imbecility of the moguls wore him out. He was definitely ill by that time, and presently he was sent to Colorado by his doctors. He made a long and gallant fight against the malady that had menaced him for years, but it was hopeless. He died on June 14, 1938. He was a month short of forty-five years old.

The great event of his life, I think, was his marriage to the

lovely Peggy Wood in 1924. He was, for all his apparent sure-
ness of foot, a singularly modest man, and he never got over
a kind of amazement that so brilliant a figure of the stage
should be interested in him. Their marriage was very happy,
despite the long separations that were forced on them by Miss
Wood's professional engagements, which often took her to
England, and Johnny's own wanderings at home. The son
born in 1927 had a proud and doting father. There are some
shy but eloquent lines to him in " To Youth " and " Turning
Point," and even more eloquent lines to his mother.

This is no place to attempt what the pedagogues call a
definitive judgment of Weaver the poet. Perhaps the best I
can do is to quote a few lines from a review of " In American " that I printed in 1921:

> His realism is very careful; no Weaverian philosophy in-
> trudes into the song. Its language is naïve, clumsy, grammar-
> less — the vulgate of poor and hopeless folk, and yet folk who
> can feel. I think that his experiment was well worth making,
> and that he has carried it out with excellent skill. . . . He
> opens the way for a ballad literature in America, representa-
> tive of true Americans and in the American language. I be-
> lieve that this endeavor is worth ten times the heavy strivings
> of poets who know that prose has teeth, and so try to palm off
> their vague and usually preposterous ideas in the guise of
> poetry.

I add a short quotation from an excellent article by Carl
Carmer, a friend of college days, in the *Hamilton Alumni
Review:*

I feel sure that he will be set down as one of the poets of the late American renaissance which brought our poetry back from Victorian artificiality to the natural and beautiful vernacular, and as a forerunner of the important group of contemporary American writers who find injustices in our national life and want to influence their readers to correct them.

Maybe this last deserves a certain qualification. Johnny was surely no uplifter, and the labored snuffling of the proletarian bards of recent vintage must have aroused his derision. But all the same he opened the way for them, and showed them all of their better tricks.

H. L. MENCKEN

Baltimore, January, 1939.

Contents

IN AMERICAN

FINDERS

MORE "IN AMERICAN"

TO YOUTH

TURNING POINT

CONTENTS

TRIAL BALANCE

※ IN AMERICAN ⊱

" Nothin' or everythin', it's got to be,"
   You says, and hides your face down on my arm.
   " If it meant nothin', 'twouldn't do no harm,
Or either everythin' — but this way — see? . . ."

I feel your tremblin' heart against my coat,
   And the big arc-light moon grins down so cool,
   " Go on! " I think it says, " you softie fool! " . . .
I love you so it hurts me in my throat. . . .

" Don't make me kiss you; sure, I know you could,"
   You're pleadin', " And we gone too far for play;
   I care a lot . . . but yet not so's to say
I love you yet. . . . Aw, help me to be good! " . . .

Oh, darlin', darlin', can't you let it be
Nothin' to you, and everythin' to me?

I wished I'd took the ring, not the Victrola.
You get so tired of records, hearin' an' hearin' 'em,
And when a person don't have much to spend
They feel they shouldn't ought to be so wasteful.
And then these warm nights makes it slow inside,
And sittin's lovely down there by the lake
Where him and me would always use ta go.

He thought the Vic'd make it easier
Without him; and it did at first. I'd play
Some jazz-band music and I'd almost feel
His arms around me, dancin'; after that
I'd turn out all the lights, and set there quiet
Whiles Alma Gluck was singin', " Home, Sweet Home,"
And almost know his hand was strokin' my hand.

" If I was you, I'd take the Vic," he says,
" It's somethin' you can use; you can't a ring.
Wisht I had ways ta make a record for you,
So's I could be right with you, even though
Uncle Sam had me." . . . Now I'm glad he didn't;
It would be lots too much like seein' ghosts
Now that I'm sure he never won't come back. . . .

Oh, God! I don't see how I ever stand it!
He was so big and strong! He was a darb!

4

The swellest dresser, with them nifty shirts
That fold down, and them lovely nobby shoes,
And always all his clothes would be one color,
Like green socks with green ties, and a green hat,
And everything. . . . We never had no words
Or hardly none. . . .

                 And now to think that mouth
I useta kiss is bitin' into dirt,
And through them curls I useta smooth, a bullet
Has went. . . .

          I wisht it would of killed me, too. . . .

Oh, well . . . about the Vic. . . . I guess I'll sell it
And get a small ring anyways. (I won't
Get but a half as good a one as if
He spent it all on that when he first ast me.)
It don't seem right to play jazz tunes no more
With him gone. And it ain't a likely chanst
I'd find nobody ever else again
Would suit me, or I'd suit. And so a little
Quarter of a karat, maybe, but a real one
That I could sparkle, sometimes, and remember
The home I should of had. . . .

             And still, you know,
The Vic was his idea, and so. . . .

                 I wonder. . . .

5

Pardon me, lady, but I wanta ast you
For God's sake, stop that tappin'. I'll go nuts,
Plain bug-house if I hear that " Tap-tap-tap "
Much longer! . . .

                  Now I went and used such langwidge
I got to tell you why. . . . Well, in the first place
My business is all shot. Now drugs theirselves
Don't pay much, and the extry stuff, like candy,
Cigars and stationery and et cetery
Don't make their keep. And that damn soda-fountain —
Excuse me, lady, but I just can't help it! . . .

Some day I'm gointa catch the guy I bought it off.
I'm losin' money every day it's here.
And soda-jerkers — now I can't get none
For love or money, so myself I got to
Mess with them malted milks, banana splits
And slop like that. And just as doggone sure
As I start workin' on some fine prescription,
The kind I love to mix, got to be careful,
The weights is hittin' on that perfect balance —
Why then some fool wants a marshmallow sundae,
And, " Tap-tap-tap " he starts in on the showcase,
And taps and taps 'til I come runnin' out,
Leavin' the drugs half-done. . . .

And that ain't all;
Here's the big trouble: I can't talk good grammar.
People don't think a man that mixes drugs
Can do it right, and talk the way I do.
It makes me sick. Why have I got to sound
Like a school teacher? Why, I know my stuff.
"Registered Pharmacist," see? I taught myself
Workin' at night whiles I was four years clerkin'.
And then I took three months down at the U,
And passed a fine exam. But here's the thing:
I quit the public school in seventh grade,
And never paid no attention to my talk.
So it's the way I tell you: they're suspicious
Because I use such slang. I try to stop
But it's too late now. I found out too late. . . .

I got a dream of what I'll do some day:
I want to quit this drug stuff altogether,
Have a nice office, with a big oak desk,
And sell just real estate. I'd like to bet
I'd make a clean-up at it. It'd be swell,
That office. . . .

But this life is killin' me,
It's the fool questions they keeps askin' me.
You see that clock there? Well, just on a guess
Three times an hour some silly fish comes in here
And calls me out, and asts me, "Is that right?
Is your clock right?" — Honest to Heaven, lady,
One day I got so sore I took a hammer
And smashed the face in. And it cost twelve dollars
To fix it. But I had peace for a week. . . .

7

Oh, gosh, my nerves! . . . But that's the way it is.

I'm sorry I spoke so rough about that tappin',
But when I get to sellin' real estate
They'll be no place where folks can take a coin
And tap, and tap 'til I come runnin' out.
That's a man's business! . . .

                              If I ever get it. . . .

Au Revoir

Don't kiss me! Not no more! . . . Oh, can't you see?
   Everythin's perfect now, the way it is.
   Why do I hafta fight and beg like this?
It's been so sweet — oh, can't you leave things be?

Oh, now I hurt you! Dear, don't look so sad. . . .
   Ah, gee, I guess men ain't got ways to know
   How a girl feels, and when it's time to go,
And how too much of even kisses is bad.

But it's the things you didn't just quite do,
   And what's left over for some other day
   That makes her wonder and hope and cry and pray,
And tell herself, "Next time!" and dream of you.

Good night, dear . . . you must go . . . it's for your
     sake. . . .
I'll dream about that kiss you didn't take. . . .

Oh, God, that dwellest 'way up there,
I want to pray a bran-new prayer.
It ain't the kind I useta say
To make me be good every day;
It ain't the kind my mother taught,
It's somethin' that I shouldn't ought —
It's selfish — maybe bad — but oh,
Listen — God — I love him so!

I guess Thou knows it any way,
But this is what I want ta say:
Make me so wonderful that he
Can't think of nothin' else but me!
Make my lips red just like wine,
Gi' my hair a golden shine,
Gi' my eyes a lovely light,
Make my body round and white. . . .

God, it can't be wicked of me
Beggin' Thee to make him love me,
Is it, God? I know I never
Felt this way before, or ever
Dreamt no man would come along
Makin' my heart beat like a song —
God, this love that come to me
Is just like when I think of Thee! . . .

Let him love just me alone,
Make him be my very own!
I guess that's lots to ast, but oh,
God, — dear God — I love him so! . . .

Amen. . . .

When I was a kid, on a fresh Spring day
I useta go at sun-up to get the smell o' May;
And say! The waves o' perfumes that they would always be!
All the flowers in the world, so it looked to me,
Was mixed with the good ol' fresh-dug ground —
A kind of smell that God his self would like to have around.

I couldn't find the smell o' the Spring today.
Somethin' is happened — took it clean away.
The same kinda apple-blooms was shinin' on the tree —
I guess it ain't the Spring changed — it must be me.
Take my money — take my house — every single thing —
Oh, Mr. Yesterday! — Let me smell the Spring!

Dénouement

So now I get the dirty throwdown, huh?
What do I mean? Yeh, that's a good one, ain't it?
How do you get that way? You think I'm blind?
I seen you with that girl the other night!

Aw, Frank, how could ya ever come to do it?
I ain't changed, am I? Ain't I just as swell?
Don't my eyes shine the same way, just for you?
Don't you remember out to old San Soozy
We win long-distance prizes, dancin' together?
You says, " You keep the prize; what's mine is yourn,
And vicey versy." Yes, and don't you remember
When you — when you first kissed me in Jim's Ford,
And all them lovely things you says to me,
And me believin' 'em, because I loved you? . . .

I should of knew, I should of knew, I should of!
Men is the same, kiddin' a girl along,
Makin' her love 'em, till she lost her brains
And done what never can't be undid now!

But still. . . .
                That night the stars was winkin' down,
And looked so bright and happy, just like me.
The little waves was chucklin' 'round the boat,
You and the wind took turns, kissin' my forrid.

13

Down underneath I felt the engines pumpin'
Just like your heart, pressin' against my cheeks.

The lights was out, it was so dark and haunted,
I felt so safe with them big arms around me,
And dreamy, with the niggers singin' soft,
Playin' their yukalalies. And I says, —
Don't you remember what I says? I says,
" See them two rows o' lights along the shore?
Them is the city's teeth, shinin' so white;
The city's laughin', just like you and me;
Laughin' and laughin'. Everybody's glad." . . .

The fool I was! The stupid, crazy fool!
I listened to your talk, give in to you,
Lovin' you heart and soul, never went home
Till noon, lied to 'em all — and now — and now —

I'm finished! — Thrun away! . . . Them lights *was* teeth,
The teeth the city's got, to tear and tear me —
Murderin', tearin' teeth! They got me in 'em! . . .

Go on away! I never want to see you!
Go get that red-head fool, tell her I sent you!
I hope she'll be another fool like me, —
I hope you burn and burn in Hell!

                            I hope —
Oh, what's there anything to hope for, now? . . .

" In love," you tells me, " I'm in love again.
    Say, he's a reg'lar doll! Some boy-chum! Oh,
    I'm wild about him! — " And you go on so
The way you always rave about your " men."

In love! The nerve! Why, on'y just last week
    It was a jackie; and the week before
    That willy-boy down to the dry-goods store —
You make me sick so I can't hardly speak!

Why, when love hits you, everythin's a dream,
    It's like you took some dope, and nothin's real
    Except one face you just can't help but see

Wakin' or sleepin' . . . All the time you scheme
    How you could help him . . . work . . . or lie . . . or
        steal,
    Die, even. . . . And you squawk " In love " to me! . . .

Don't look like that! You know I druther die
   Than hurt you, ever, any. But it wouldn't
   Be but a worst hurt after, and I couldn't
Say nothin' else that wouldn't be a lie.

It's a queer sorter way that I love you —
   A kinder quiet, happy peace you bring,
   Like after a rainstorm hearin' a robin sing —
But it ain't the flamin' way you want me to.

God knows I tried, and even tried to kiss you
   And find it that way, but it wasn't real —
   They wasn't that fire I always hoped I'd feel. . . .
So . . . it's good-bye. . . . Oh, God, I'm goin' to miss you,

The way you smile, the little things you say. . . .
But Truth is Truth. . . . They ain't no other way. . . .

Well, boys, that's twicet I win. I leave it lay.
"The works or nothin'" — that's me every time.
Four Jewish flags I blow, four lovely bucks.
It's sugar in your mouth! — How's that? All set? —
Go get 'em, dices! — Wham! — Read 'em and weep! . . .

Oh, Snake-eyes, acety-ace — you done me wrong!
Craps, and I lose the works. . . . All right, I'm through.
It ain't no use to buck the jinx, but listen,
Brother, I may be right in a few minutes,
And when I am — look out for your gol' teeth.

My motter's "play 'em hard or else not any."
I got no use at all for these here pikers
That drags down every time they makes a pass.
A piker is a guy that plays it safe,
And that's the place I'll say they always ends,
Safe where they started in. You tell 'em, brother.

Don't get me wrong, though. All the flops is full
O' suckers that takes a chanst on anythin'.
You gotta use judgment. But a piker, now,
They got no faith in nothin', not even theirself.

Dick Finch, he was a goof like what I mean.
Well, this bird has a job down to a shoe store,

17

Gets just enough to keep his bones together,
And keeps the same job seven straight-on years
Without no raise. He come to me one day
And spills a moanin' howl. It was like this,
He says, his old man keeps a little store
Out to the West Side, sellin' fruit and such.
Now they's a mortgage on it, comin' due,
And if he can't raise six hunderd cold bucks
By three weeks from that day, his Pa is ruint.

I stands there for a minute. Then I says,
" How much dough do you think that you can raise
Right now? " He fishes in his pockets then,
And hauls me out a roll o' dirty bills.

" Thirty-three dollars. All I saved this year."

" Now, listen, Bud, just how much do you care
About your Pa? Enough to take a chanst
On losin' all o' this to save his neck? "

He gulps, and nods his head. " You bet I do."

" Well, then, I'm gonna give you somep'n straight.
This dough is all you got. You got no ways
O' gettin' hold o' no six hunderd dollars,
Not with no job like yourn. They's just one way:
You go down to the track this afternoon.

" Now in the third race, they's a dog name Lucas.
Two birds I know has got that mule in pickle,
And somep'n tells me today's the day

18

They set to make a killin'. Nobody knows
Exceptin' me and them about him, see?
I got a-plenty right now on his nose.
You go down there, and find the nearest bookie,
And put the whole roll on this skate — to win!"

He sorter trembles "What, the whole darn roll?"

"That's what I said, you hearn me," answers me.
"If I ain't right, you lose. But even then
Your Pa ain't no worse off than he is now.
And it's a good tip what I'm givin' you.
The odds you get'll be twenty to one,
And if that plater romps in to the merry,
You draw down what you need, six hunderd frog-skins,
And sixty more besides. . . . Now I ain't sayin'
That this is no sure thing. But it's a chanst,
And a durn good one. So hop to it, fella,
And just this one time say, 'The works or nothin'.'"

Honest, you should of saw what this bird done.
I thought the pore durn simp was goin' to kiss me.
I give him a shove, and off he puts a-runnin'.

That night I seen this Finch down to the poolroom.
I walks right up and clouts him on the back.
"Well, sport, we sorter knocked 'em for a gool.
I'll tell the world we did — why, what's the matter?"
I looks again. This Finch starts in to blubber,
"Oh, God! — Oh, God! —" and he can't get no further.

I grabs his shoulders, gives him one good shake.
"Say, what the what?" I says. "This 'Lucas' win.
He walks in backwards, like I told you, don't he?   ·

19

What're you yellin' about? Your Pa is saved,
You got a nest-egg over, too — but wait —
You went there, didn't you?"

                        "Yeh, I went," he blubbers.
"I seen the prices — 'Lucas, twenty to one.'
I has my money in my hand, and walks up
And gets right to the bookie — then a somep'n
It seems to scare me. I gets thinkin' how
Everythin' that I got is in my hand.
And sorter sudden-like my knees starts tremblin',
And then — I guess I must of gotten crazy
Just for a minute, and —"

                     "Go on, go on!"
I hollers, feelin' sick.

                 "Oh, God — I done
Like what I allus do — I took and bought
A two-buck ticket for this horse to show,
Just as the bettin' closed." . . .

                    Well, can you beat it?
I guess a piker oncet, a piker forever.
It's in the blood, you see! . . .

                Gimme them bones!

Why're you always pullin' sob-stuff?
  Honey, what's the big idear?
"Will I never love no others? —
  How many girls do I get a year?"
What's the good o' borryin' trouble?
  Damn tomorrow! What's it worth?
Just this lovin' night can give us
  Everythin' there is on earth.

Say, you know old Apple Annie,
  Blurry-eyes, and nose all blue?
Oncet she was a knock-out looker,
  Oncet she was as sweet as you.
While she's creepin' 'round the alleys
  Why d'ye think she smiles all day?
'Cause her old bean's all chuck full with
  Things no years can't take away.

Kiss me like you want to kiss me,
  Lock your arms around me tight!
Don't be fightin' what you're feelin' —
  Nothin' matters but tonight!
When you're dry, and white, and pinched-up
  You'll remember times like this —
You'll be glad and glad, I tell you,
  For the joys you didn't miss.

Say — listen —
If you could only take a bath in moonlight!

Hey! Can't you just see yourself
Take a runnin' dive
Inta a pool o' glowin' blue,
Feel it glidin' over you
All aroun' and inta you —

Grab a star — huh? —
Use it for soap;
Beat it up to bubbles
And white sparklin' foam —
Roll and swash —

Gee!

I just like to bet
You could wash your soul clean
In moonlight!

You take a dog, oncet you get it to love you,
You lose your home, your dough, your grub and all,
The old dog sticks. . . . A cat's a different critter,
More like a slot-machine: put in a meal
You get a purr right back; no meal, no purr —
Claws, prob'ly; then, " So long." . . .

                                        I'll take a cur.

Push the screen back just a little more
So's I can hear 'em playin' " To the Color."
Wisht I could see the boys, clickin' their heels smart,
All glad and clean, neat fer Retreat, after the day's sweat.

Here's me in bed — God, what a joke, —
Me that wanted to fight, knowin' I gotta croak, —
Don't kid me, Doc, the head's burnin' up —
I know, Doc — I know.

I left my job, six bucks a day,
Expert lathe hand, that was me.
Told 'em I hated the Dutch, wanted to carry a gun,
Drilled, drilled, drilled,
Gets hard as nails — then a order come —

" Expert lathe hand, Richard H. Jones
Transferred at oncet." So I come here
Down to the Audience corps — me that wanted to fight —
They takes my gun, gives me a shovel.

Audience corps, right — all my buddies gone
Scrappin' over seas, me left to watch,
Watch — and dig latrines.

" Jones, lathe hand, what the bloomin' Hell,"
So the C. O. says, " No place for you

Just yet awile. Here's a shovel, Jones,
You do your bit — dig, Jones, dig! — "

That's the way it is, me that wanted to fight
Stuck in a hole here,
Diggin' — God! — latrines!

Good ol' army, huh?

Still, I suppose
Somebody knows
What's the big idear, and I guess a guy
Can fight for what he loves,
And do his damned bit,
Yeh, and die for it —

Even with a shovel.

There was me, walkin' peaceful down the alley,
Smokin' a pipe. The sun was blazin' down,
It was all quiet, like any reg'lar noon-day.
I squats down on a bar'l, lights a match,
And, " Bang-bang-bang! " I hears, and drops the pipe.

A guy runs at me, hollers, " You! Where is he?
You seen him! " I just sets there. " Keep your shirt on,"
I says. " Where's who? "

                         " The Nigger! Where's he at? "
They gangs around me. I just sets there dumb.
More on 'em runs up, yelpin' " Get the coon."
They jams aroun' the cellar; they's a yell,
They dashes down the steps. . . . A dozen shots. . . .
The white guy next me pitches up his mitts
And flops down. . . . Then. . . .

                     Listen, I wanta ast you,
You been down to the zoo, feedin' time?
You seen the keeper thrun a hunk o' steak,
You hearn the awful snarl the tigers gi'n?
. . . That mob. . . .

                 They drags this moanin' nigger out,
They kicks his face in right before my eyes,

They plugs him full o' bullets,
What's left ain't even quiverin' no more.
I seen it, me. The wagon comes a-clangin',
Nobody left but me to tell about it,
Me and the half-killed bum. . . .

                        And now you come,
Tryin' to make me swear before a judge
This pore old alley-cat was goin' gunnin',
And murderin' white guys. . . .

I s'pose I was a dumb-bell. That's what Mame said,
Least wise she didn't say it in them words,
But " dumb-bell " — that was what she meant, all right,
And all because I couldn't understand her.

But what can you do with a girl that wants to set
Out on a rock and watch the waves come up,
Right in plain daylight? And you're talkin' to her,
And all at oncet she says, " Can't you keep quiet?
Can't you see the waves is whisperin' secrets at me? " . . .
— If she wouldn't of been so wonderful to look at,
And so darn sweet the few times that she *was* sweet,
I wouldn't never fooled with her at all.
But that's the funny thing. The more I seen her,
And the more she went off into — you know — fits
Like she was miles away, the more I wanted her. . . .

Here's one trick I put up with from this Mame.
One time at ten p. m. she comes to the house,
Says, " Get your heavy coat, we're goin' ridin'."
" Ridin'," I says. " Say, Mame, what's eatin' you?
A blizzard's outside, and the worst this year."
" Shut up. Come on," she says, and drags me out.
We rides two hours in a open hansom, —
I guess it was one that Noah had in the ark —
The snow just stingin' and beatin' on our face,

And all because Mame never done it before,
And seen the cab, and wanted to. She said
It was a real adventure. . . . I got chilblains. . . .

What can you do when you take a girl to dinner,
And she goes and orders — heck — of all things — snails!
And when I ast her to a real good show,
She makes me change it to some darn grand oprer,
And won't set downstairs, but she has to stay
Up in the Peanut Gallery, with the Dagoes.

I sure did stand a lot! . . . She was bad enough
In the city; but when she got out to the country
She sure complete went wild. If she seen a field
Where they was grass and flowers, she takes a run
And jumps and rolls aroun'; and not just her,
She makes me do it, too. I was so shamed,
It wasn't right, us bein' so old, you might say. . . .

And one time towards evenin' we was walkin',
And come to a little crick. The fish was jumpin',
And right away she says, " I want to fish! "
We couldn't fish, I argues, there wasn't no poles,
Nor hooks, nor lines nor nothin'. She says, " Hush.
I got a pin. You bend it on a rock,
I'll get a line, all right. Go on and bend it."
Whiles I was turned aroun', I hears a rip,
She hands me a long piece of her underskirt,
Honest, it made me blush. She breaks a stick off,
And catches a grasshopper, and she fishes.
And what do you think? She catched a fish, at that,
A thing about two inches long. And say,
I thought it was a whale, the fuss she made.

She was so happy, I didn't know what to think,
And afterwards we laid down on a haystack,
And she was watchin' the stars, and sorter hummin',
So sweet I got a notion it was me
That she was singin' about, and I tried to kiss her.
That sure was one bum guess. She turns all white,
And says, " All right, you had to ruin it.
I might of knew." And then we went back home,
Her starin' straight ahead, and sayin' nothin'. . . .

And then, the next day, she was fine again.

I couldn't tell what she was ever thinkin'.
Things went on that way, me bein' her dog,
You might say, tryin' to bust away, and yet
All the time comin' back. So then, one day,
I swore I'd have a showdown. I was through
With all this foolin'. Either I was right
Or either wrong, and I was goin' to find out.

I ast her to eat lunch with me at Schlogel's.
I gets there first, all set up and excited,
And in a minute here she comes, all fixed up,
Prettier'n a little red wagon. We sets down,
And " That's a nice new suit. How good you look,"
Says Mame, and so I'm feelin' fine, right off,
And she is wonderful, laughin' and talkin',
So's I can't hardly wait to say my spiel.

I orders, and the waiter beats it. Then
I clears my throat, and looks at her, and starts,
" Mame, I got somethin' that I want to ast you —

30

Mame — " And I starts to lean 'way over to her,
And finds my pants is ruined.
What do you think?
Some boob has stuck a great big wad of gum
Right to the chair, and I was settin' in it!

You know, I got so mad I couldn't think.
I clean forgets all I was tryin' to say,
And hollers " Damn it! " . . . There was my new suit
All ruined with that gum. Mame busts out laughin',
And when she laughs I'm gettin' all the sorer.

Then she gets sore, too. " What's a little thing
Like that," she says. " You ack just like a kid! "
Maybe I did, but who's the guy that wouldn't?
I calls the manager, and bawls him out
Like any guy would do.

                    And suddenly
Mame she gets right up, and she sorter smiles
And says, " Good-bye. And this is real good-bye.
Charley, you'll never learn to really live
Unless you get so little hurts don't matter.
Life is too big to let a thing like gum
Mean such a lot to you." . . . And out she sails.
I calls her up next day. She tells me no,
She found that her and me can't hit it off.

" Here's the whole truth: You drag me down," she says.
" You don't know how to dream, and never won't.
That's all. Good-bye."

31

I can't just understand about the Fall.
　Why, everythin's so wild and bright and gay!
It's like the world was at a Fancy Ball,
　And nothin' mattered excep' just to play.

The birds is singin' crazy bran-new tunes;
　The bushes got red ribbons for their hair;
The trees looks like they bought theirself balloons,
　Scarlet and yellow wavin' in the air.

They know they got old Winter fooled, I s'pose.
　And though he'll come some day, and tear and roar,
Bust up their party, ruin their pretty clo'es,
　It'll be all right when Spring comes back once more.

And still, it makes me all choke up, to know
All lovely things that's now, has got to go.

Headlines

(*Easter Sunday, April, 1918*)

They's headlines snarlin' at me from the " Journal,"
" Hun Drive Slows."
Slows! And I prayed last night it was stopped!
A robin just hopped
On top of a red-bud tree,
Looks to me like a rose
That a girl's holdin' up next to her cheek. . . .
   Or maybe like that liquid fire them Germans uses. . . .

Clink! — Clink! —
The sidewalks is ringin' from the feet
Of folks goin' to church, all neat,
Gettin' ready to split their voice
Singin', " Rejoice! Rejoice!
He is risen! "
Like a man outa prison
The vi'lets is bustin' outa the ground. . . .
The headlines I'm starin' at jumps and lurches:
" Mystery Gun Slays Crowds
Prayin' in Paris Churches." . . .

Here comes a young sojer
With a girl hangin' onto his arm.
Right here only a year ago Jim useta walk
And him and me would useta talk

All about the glories o' fightin' for your country. . . .
" Airman Falls in Gallant Fight " —

That was Jim's headline. . . . I was Jim's girl. . . .
Just such a light
He useta have in his face,
Just like that he had a sorter grace
When he walked. . . . Just like that
His hair useta curl. . . .

Apple-blossoms is ridin' along on the breeze,
Flutterin' down from the trees
Like a sweet-smellin' snow —
Or like frost on them graves in Picardy. . . .

Oh, God!

Good God, almighty God,
Are you gonna stand by
And let all the things that was beautiful die?
Them Huns is killin' even the Spring,
Every little no-account lovely thing,
Twistin' everythin' inta pain. . . .

Oh, God,
Won't Beauty never come no more again! . . .

Say, Ma, I want to tell you about Pa.
We got to have a new deal in this house.
I ain't gonna stand no more o' his fool talk.

Don't bust in on me. I know what I'm doin'.
This ain't no new idear. Many a time
I been about to say it, only now
I come to where it's gettin' on my nerves.
He's like a phonograft with just one record,
And he keeps playin' it, over and over and over.

Seems like the first stuff I can ever remember
Is all that bunk about a " edjucation,"
Pa bein' fixed to go down to the U,
And then his Pa dies, and he goes to work
To keep old Gramma goin'. " Will," he says,
" I never got the thin' I wanted most.
But never mind, you'll get it, Will, you'll get it.
My son is goin' to be a college man.
I'm savin' all the time a College Fund."

Remember how he always talked that way?
And then the day I went down to the High School
He give me a swell new watch, and pats my shoulder,
And says, " Good boy, Will, now you got the system.
Plug at the books, and plug, and keep a-pluggin;
They's stuff in books you can't get nowhere else,

35

Stuff that'll give you dreams, and that's what counts;
Men that can dream is the ones that beats the world."

The first time that I got real good and sore
Was when he points me out that Freddy Keefe,
And says he hopes that I should be like that.
Why should I want to be a sorter mouse,
Nice enough feller, but a-scared to fight
Or play, or nothin' else but fool with books?
I couldn't help if I was born the way
I was, and liked to run around, and hated
Latin, and that damn Algebra, and so on.
But even then I might of gotten through
If he wouldn't of give me a lickin' for not passin'
Into the third year High. That spilled the beans.
I only stuck that long because I knowed
How much it meant to him. But gettin' licked —
You said yourself you didn't blame me much
For beatin' it the way I did, and bummin'
Down into Texas. . . . Talk about " edjucation "!
I seen more in one year than lots o' guys
'Ll ever see if they lives to be a hunderd.

Pa knows I wasn't never any burden.
I earned my keep and more, didn't I, now?
I useta feel kinder sorry now and then,
Special the time I found the old bank book,
And ast him what would he do with the College Fund
He was still keepin', though I was sixteen then,
And he says he didn't know, but maybe hoped
They was a chanst I'd change my mind some day.

I guess he thought I was a just plain bum.
It sorter socked him when he ast Sam French
Where I was workin' and repairin' autos,
And Sam tells him I was the best repair man
On the West Side.

                And when I comes and tells him
I wants to borry the College Fund to use
For capital to start my own garage,
I swear I think he cried when he give it to me.
He needn't been that way. I paid it back,
Yeh, and I give him interest, eight per cent.
It didn't take me only two years to do it.

Look what I done for you and him and me!
Though I ain't the one to say it, do you know
Where they's another guy that's twenty-seven
And makes the dough I make? All in six years
I built a fine big house, I got a Packard
To ride you in, and business is boomin'
So's now I aim to open up three branches.

And here last night this Freddy Keefe comes over,
And him and Pa is gassin' roun' the fire.
A fine, hot-lookin' bird this Freddy is,
With his suit shinin', and his scuffed-up shoes,
Tellin' me how he loved his work and all,
Him a perfesser, tryin' to teach a gang
O' shell-shocks how to read and write and such.

And when I shows him all my new silk shirts
He sorter smiles, and says, " You're lucky, Will.

37

I won't get a new overcoat this winter;
I bought a season ticket to the concerts."
And then him tellin' Pa about some painter
That had a exposition in the Institute —
All about Whoozis, some new Irish pote,
And somethin' about the " grace o' Grecian sculpcher."

The grace o' my cat's ankle! Edjucation!
That's all the good his learnin' done for him.
He ain't got nothin', and he never won't have.
I couldn't listen to that line o' bunk,
So I just starts the player-piano goin',
And Freddy says good-bye and goes away.

That's when Pa comes and has the nerve to tell me
I shoulda listened to Freddy. " I just tell you,"
He says. " You needn't be so rude to Freddy.
He's gettin' a repitation everywhere."
" For what? For shiny clo'es? " I comes back, laughin'.
Pa's face gets red. " No, for a lit'ry cricket."
" Haw haw," I says. " He sure chirps mighty feeble."

That's when Pa makes the break that gets my goat.
" Well, you can laugh," he says, " But just the same
I'd give the world if you was only like him."

Just think o' that! Now, honest, can you tie it?
Me, that'll be a real rich man some day,
Trade places with a teacher! With a bum
That scarcely gets a good square meal a week!
Concerts, and pitchers — yeh, and I spose pink teas.

38

All right, if that's the kinda things Pa wants
He can get out and find it. I won't keep him,
And feed him swell, and dress him swell, and give him
A great big room, and rides in bran-new Packards.

If he wants what this Freddy Keefe is got,
By God, he's got to get it somewhere's elset.
But I ain't goin' to hear no more about it.

You tell him this for me — tell him I mean it:
Either he shuts his trap and keeps it shut
About this edjucation stuff, or elset
He can get the Hell out of here.

That's all!

When Jake played his cornet, his face
    Looked like a catfish when you land him;
We called him " Catfish " Green, and laughed,
    And never tried to understand him.

He sawed and hammered at his bench
    Without a word or smile, all day;
But when night come, he'd get that horn
    And be a changed man, right away.

I see him now, when he'd oblige
    With " Silver Threads Among — " you know —
His fingers lovin' at the keys,
    The long notes wailin' smooth and low.

That was great stuff. But when he led
    The concerts with the other boys
Down to the square, in summer-time,
    Why, Hell ain't never hearn such noise.

They squawked and blared, and lost the time —
    We laughed until we almost died.
But " Catfish " — he would yell and swear —
    And oncet he broke down flat, and cried.

Still, through three years, two times a week
    He made that awful band rehearse,

And never seemed to realize
  It never got no good, but worse.

And then, one day the news flew round,
  " On July Fourth our town will be
Host to our country's President " —
  Jake grinned, and muttered, " Now you'll see! "

And every night that June we heard
  Them trombones' snarls and cornets' ravin's;
The cashier of the Farmers' Bank
  Said Jake had drawed out all his savin's.

The great day come. And down the road
  A bust o' music, like a storm,
And here comes " Catfish," with his band
  Each in a brand-new uniform!

Jake and the boys struts on the stand —
  Good Lordy! What a high-tone manner!
The Pres'dent halts. The band explodes
  Into the " Star Spangled Banner."

Never no band played like that day,
  It sure did make my pulses jump.
Jake takes the high note sweet and clear —
  And sinks down with a little thump.

The music stops — they lifts him up —
  One little sigh, and Jake is dead.
That high-note climax of his life
  Bust a blood-vessel in his head.

.   .   .   .   .

41

Well, at that time, to my kid mind
   Thinkin' o' Jake, it sure did seem
A foolish way to waste a life
   Chasin' a silly sort o' dream.

But now I kinder guess I hope
   The Lord will treat me that way, too.
I'll gladly go, like " Catfish " Green,
   Knowin' I made my dream come true.

Oh, yes, I spose a day has got to come
   That gets around to all of us at last,
That Springtime won't mean much excep' a season,
   And April nights won't make our heart beat fast.

And we can watch the long green rollers breakin',
   And be real pleased to stay all safe on shore —
Nothin' but catchin' colds, or wearin' rubbers,
   Or things like that'll matter any more.

And glad or sad times that we useta feel so,
   And hopes and thrills that we could find in looks,
And how a kiss could burn us like a fire —
   They'll be like stuff we read about in books.

Let's don't be like the others — scared or sour,
   Forgettin' that life wasn't always slow,
Growlin' at fun and dancin' and happy laughin',
   Snoopin' and spyin' 'round, and snarlin', " No! "

Promise that you'll be different! — not like them! —
   Fight for the ways of seein' fresh and true!
Keep all you can of what the world meant to you
   When you was young, and life was real . . . and new!

FINDERS

"Finders in the dark, you Steve with a dinner bucket,
  you Steve clumping in the dusk on the sidewalks with
  an evening paper for the woman and kids, you Steve
  with your head wondering where we all end up —

"Finders in the dark, Steve: I hook my arm in cinder
  sleeves; we go down the street together; it is all the
  same to us; you Steve and the rest of us end on the
  same stars; we all wear a hat in hell together, in hell
  or heaven." —

SMOKE AND STEEL,
by Carl Sandburg

I'm comin' back and haunt you, don't you fret.
   What if I get as far as Hell away?
   They's things of me that just can't help but stay —
Whether I want or not, you can't forget.

Just when you think you got me wiped out clear,
   Some bird that's singin' — moonlight on a hill —
   Some lovely thing'll hurt like it would kill,
And you'll hear somethin' whisperin', " He's here! "

And when somebody holds you closte, like this,
   And you start in to feel your pulses race,
   The face that's pressin' yours'll be my face . . .
My lips'll be the ones your lips'll kiss.

Don't cry . . . which do you think it'll hurt most? —
Oh, God! You think I want to be a ghost? . . .

Every mornin' I useta watch and wonder,
   While all them pigeons was flyin' around his head,
What was he doin' with that, now, fishin'-pole,
   Funny and black-like, and the sky all red.

After a while, I thought he must be crazy:
   Didn't he know they don't catch birds that way?
But still he done it, and I finely goes
   Inta the bird-store, and I asts 'em, " Say,

" That dizzy gink there, 'way up on the roof,
   What is he doin'? What's he tryin' to prove? "
They says he was a reg'lar pigeon-scarer,
   And has to keep them pigeons on the move.

A pigeon is a lazy thing, you see?
   They like to set around, and hate to fly;
But if you let 'em, then they clean forget
   How flyin' is, and so get sick, and die

Now ain't that funny? But I got to thinkin'
   How Life is like that. And, you know, it seems
Troubles and things like those is pigeon-scarers,
   And pigeons is your soul, or elset your dreams.

If everything goes right, they get all lazy,
   And fat, and crawl around all weak and slack;

48

So then old pigeon-scarer comes along,
　　And pokes 'em up. And all the stren'th comes back

Into your dream-wings or your soul-wings — see? —
　　And — whish! — they leave the lazy parts of you
Down on the ground; and up, 'way up they go,
　　Up where it's clean, and beautiful, and blue. . . .

But here's the sad part, when you come to think:
　　They sneak back to the place he chased 'em from.
Always they get back to the lazy ways —
　　Always the pigeon-scarer has to come. . . .

"Never pick wild flowers!" —
   That's what she would say,
"Leave 'em free, in the fields
   Where they can play —

"Play, and be beautiful
   Under the big sky!
If you try to take 'em home
   Wild flowers die."

Then she shook her little head,
   And I went crazy
Wantin' her, standin' there
   Like a brown-eyed daisy.

"Such talk!" I thinks then,
   "All a sweet lie!
Other people pick 'em,
   Why shouldn't I?"

If I'd only listened!
   What have I done!
"Never pick a wild love" —
   Where's my flowers gone!

"Concerning the Economic Independence of Women"

" And after all," she says, " and after all,
Daughter or not, I got my life to live,
And there ain't no one elset can live it, see?
So if I wanta do the way I wanta,
You nor nobody elset is gointa stop me.
I'm gettin' twenty per, down to the office,
And that's enough to live on, if I hafta;
Either you cut this always jawin' out,
Or either I takes my little trunk to Jane's. . . .
I just as lief to anyways, and rather,
Only I know how lonely you would be
With only Pa to talk to, and him tired
So's that he lays around and snores all evenin',
And you wore out with sewin' all day long.
But if I wanta go out twicet a week,
Or three or four times, why, that's my own business;
And where I go, and who I go there with . . .
That's my own business, too. And so, that's that! "

And then I says a awful foolish thing. . . .
I says, " Look out, Miss, or I tell your Pa."

Oh, Jim, you should of ought to see the look
She give me then, and her eyes all on fire.

" That's swell! " she says. " Yeh, I just wish you try it.
Now listen, Ma, you better get this straight:
If you sic Pa on me, and he starts in
To bawl me out, too, that's the end for sure.
Him bawl me out! Not neither of you won't."

I seen she meant it, too. So don't you never,
Not never, say a word. . . . Then I got frantic,
Seein' her standin' there, so independent
And sassy, and so beautiful, and foolish. . . .

I just broke down and cried, and tried to beg her
To not be quite so wild and act so crazy.
" Why don't you find some nice boy, and get married? "

She drawed herself up, awful proud and fierce.
"Get married! Me? Aw, Ma, don't make me laugh!
Me only nineteen, and get tied for life
To some poor fish that thinks he's gointa own me,
And tell me what to do? . . . Not for this girlie!
Nobody runs me, and nobody will.
Men is all right to fool around and play with,
But they's too many nice ones in the world
To ever stick to one. I know 'em, too,
And I can handle 'em. So you should worry."

What could I do? I begs her, I just begs.
" Helen, my darlin' kiddie, can't you see?
I ain't a-scoldin', I'm just tryin' to show you.
I know you ain't a bad girl, nor you won't be.
But all this runnin' to cabarets and dancin',
And takin' drinks, I guess, and auto-ridin' . . .
It all seems fine and lively and excitin'.

" ' This is the life! ' you says the other day.
And kissin' ain't no harm, so far as that goes,
Nor anything — not anything that's real.
But that ain't real — that stuff all you is doin' . . .
It's cheap — just cheap, I tell you, and it wastes you.
Them pretty cheeks 'll fade and in a while
You'll get so sick and tired of excitement
It won't excite no more. And all the mystery
From everything 'll go. And even moonlight . . .
Oh, I know how it is, I can remember. . . .
Even the moonlight 'll look pale and sick-like.
And then, the things that might have meant so much, . . .
Real love, and pretty things, 'll be all stale
And tiresome — just stale. Oh, won't you see?
For God's sake, have you got to eat your cake
All in one bite, and not have nothin' left?
Those is the rules — they ain't no way to beat 'em. . . .
You sure can't eat your cake, and have it, too! "

Oh, Jim, she turns away, and humps her shoulders,
And says, " Well, Ma, you said your speech, I hope?
Old people always thinks and talks that way.
I'm sorry, but you know it's my own life.
And don't belong to nobody but me.
So long, and don't set up too late to-night. . . .
I guess I won't be back till two or three." . . .

The moon has gone to her bed to-night,
And all over the sky
She has hung out her garments of light
To dry.

And now each shimmering veil —
Sea-greens and sapphires,
Jeweled with orange fires —
Floats from the star she has pinned it to. . . .

I think I saw her, at the day's break
A morning or so ago,
Washing them, down by the end of the lake,
Bending quite low,
So tired she was,
And pale. . . .

Nose

I got sharp eyes, yeh? And my hands moves quick.
You got to be that way, if the sea is where
You live and work and hope to die. That's me.
And eyes and hands is fine; but listen here:
The thing that made me what I am to-day
Is just this funny thing I call my nose.

You hardly ever hear a nose get credit
Except in tunes about vi'lets and roses,
Or mother bakin' pies, or leaves that's burnin'.
But them is easy smells. The hard ones is
The kind that makes a difference in your life.

Now . . . put me back to where I'm a young kid,
Runnin' around the streets and raisin' hell.
But they's one place I just can't keep away from,
And that's the power-station for the cable.
Remember it? Corner of Clark and Ellum?
The big wheels poundin', " Rum-rum-rum! " and always
That same smell, like a knife; it's tar and oakum.
Wheels, and that stuffy, cuttin' oakum smell!

And further down, along the Clark Street bridge,
The coffee, bein' roasted in the warehouse,
And the blue smoke that give your nose a treat.

And on South Water, where the fish was laid out,
Shiny with brine, and with that salty smell
Of places that I'd only saw in dreams.
And last of all, the big ol' pumpin' station,
With fresh steam and the oil all mixed together,
And, boy, the way I used to stand and sniff,
And sniff, and let my eye ride up and down,
Up — and down — and up — with that big piston —
Say, I had lots of treats since then, but never
No treats like them when I was little and young.

Until — well, one day fifteen years from then,
When I was sellin' shoes down in Noo York,
And hatin' it, and not knowin' why I did,
It happened I went down to the docks, to see
A friend. A ship was tied up to the pier,
Unloadin' stuff. A breeze come up a-sudden,
And all to oncet I got a whoppin' whiff.
By Gee! There it was, all to oncet together:
Coffee, and fish, and salt, and steam and oakum,
And the hot oil — all in one crazy snoot-full!
And there I was — a little kid again!

So then I knowed the only kinda work
That I was made for, or could love. You see?

I shipped the very next day for a stoker,
And they ain't but damn few ports in the whole world
That I ain't stuck this nose of mine into.

Eyes? And ears? And mouth? And hands? All right;
But what I got to say, hooray for nose!
Folley your nose, I says, folley your nose! . . .

"Love 'Em and Leave 'Em"

I

Love 'em and Leave 'em — that's me, from now on.
I'm through with all this stuff about " forever " —
I'm through with ever *meanin'* it, I mean.
I'm through with tellin' nothin' but the truth,
And playin' square, and never pullin' tricks,
Or lettin' any woman get your goat
So that a man don't think about themself,
But always worries how to please or help *her*.
A bird's a sap that really falls in love —
Love 'em and Leave 'em — and to Hell with 'em.

Before I met this Nellie, I was that way;
I always had that motto, " Love 'em and leave 'em ";
I found it in some song, and say, I used it.
Kid 'em along, you know, tell 'em I cared,
Trick 'em or beat 'em — whatever it was they needed —
And if they bit, all right; and if they didn't,
All right again — they's always plenty more.

Well, then, one night, down to the corner drug-store
I and Jack Marks was soppin' up a coke,
Givin' some Janes the eye — and *she* comes in.
I come near chokin' and drops the glass right there.
Jack gives a grin, and asts, " You want to meet her? "
And so he takes me up to where she stands,

57

Makin' the other girls around look sick,
Quiet and dignified and some ways sad;
One of them undecided blondes, you know,
Sometimes bright yellow hair, sometimes it's brown;
Lively and cute, like blondes, but, at the same time,
Fires that burn and burn way deep down under . . .
But to get back to where I was, Jack wispers,
" She lives a block from me — she's pretty, ain't she?
But, boy, she ain't got time for guys like you."
She turns around, and looks up very calm;
And, in that second, all the lines I had,
All of the reg'lar lies and funny stuff
I was all set for springin', sorta choked me,
And there I was, dumb like a high-school kid.
I give one look into them big blue eyes,
And, like you'd say, I took a runnin' dive
Into 'em, and I couldn't seem to come up.
What did we say? The good Lord only knows,
Only, when I was in my room again,
There was her name down on a sheet of paper,
And me fixed up to see her the next night,
And still a swimmin', like, in them blue eyes.

II

Well, the next night I goes down to her house
And takes her to a movie. Just by luck
It was a pitcher that was kinda good;
It had some laughs, and yet it had some tears,
And some way made us feel we knew each other.
All the way home, we didn't say a lot;
But pretty soon we got down to her porch,

And she says, " Hush, let's don't make too much noise;
Let's set and talk a little w'ile: you wanta? "
Gee! That there hour — I couldn't start to tell you
The wonderful strange thing it was to me.
It was the way we was from that night on;
The realest kind of pals that ever was.
I always give her all that I could give:
And her — well, anyways, she didn't kid me,
She was more honester than most girls are.
Well, I went home that night walkin' on air,
With sleighbells ringin' in my head, and bugles,
And oh, I ain't got words to say it right.
All I can say is I was gone for fair.

And when I got down to my job, next mornin'
The boss comes by, and stops, and looks me over:
" Well, Frank, I s'pose the sky'll fall down next.
You here ahead o' time, and lookin' happy."
Boy, was I good? I made a record that day,
Sellin' eight suits, and sixteen pairs of shoes,
And the Lord knows how many other things.

The boss come round that night and wagged his head,
And, " Frank," he says, " I don't know what's got in you,
But I sure hope it stays. You keep it up.
And, pretty soon, you'll be too good for us."
But I was gone already through the door.
I grabbed some chow, and put the glad rags on,
And in another hour there was us,
Nellie and me, dancin' round at the party
The Jolly Six was givin' at Red Men's Hall.

And talk about the way them birds come round
For dances! Say, it was a mob-scene, right.
More'n a dozen must of came up to me,
And ast me where I had been hidin' her.
And, funny thing, I swear I wasn't jealous;
The better time she had, the better I had.

III

From that night on, I was her steady guy.
And, then, it come along the first of June,
And the big boss he calls me in one day,
And says, " Sit down, Frankie, I wanta see you.
You sure been makin' time around this place.
Now listen here: I'm goin' to Chicago,
And sell this store and start two new ones there.
Now I got such a crazy faith in you
I tell you what I'll do: you come with me,
I'll make you manager of one big store.
What do you say, my boy? "

What could I say?

I nearly busted tryin' to thank him right.
I grabbed my lid and beat it down to Nellie's
And finds her sittin' in the parlor there,
And spills it at her. So she says, " That's great!
Frank, I'm so proud! " And then she starts in cryin'
All of a sudden like her heart was cracked.
" Oh, Frank," she says, " What will I do without you?
What will I ever do without my boy-chum? "
I trembles like I got the Spanish flu —
Then, " Nell," I says, " Let's you and me get married! "

Nellie quit cryin', but she just sat there
And stared and stared out of the parlor window
Just like she didn't hear me. I kep' talkin',
" Nellie, I'm goin' to be a big success,
And what I'll get in Chi 'll be enough
To give you a nice home, and after a while
A lot of things. Nellie! That's what I want —
To give you things, and give 'em, and keep givin'."

I waited there, it seemed like a whole hour
For her to answer. She just went on starin'.
After a while she turned them blue eyes round
And looked a long time right straight into mine.
Then, " Frank," she says at last, " I like you fine.
You're the best friend a girl could ever have.
Always so thoughtful, always bein' nice,
But marryin' . . . and love . . . that's somethin' different.
Oh, don't you think I haven't thought about it,
Hours and hours — about love, I mean.

" And this is what I know: when love does come,
It'll be like a fire in my blood,
It'll be crazy music in my head;
The man that I would love would make me feel
Like I was weak and helpless, just to see him;
I would be scared to death, almost, and yet
It would be wonderful, that bein' scared.
Frank, you're the only person that I care for,
But . . . Frank . . . you never made me feel that way."

I couldn't say a word. I put my arm
Around her, and I kissed her on the mouth,

But it was only like I kissed a sister —
They wasn't nothin' answerin' about it.
I looks at her a minute, then I says,
" Nellie, I guess I see the way it is.
All right, I s'pose the best thing I can do
Is beat it just as far as I can get.
Thank God I got that job up in Chicago.
It'll be one way to forget you. . . . See? "
Then Nellie starts to cry all over again.
" Oh, Frank, I just can't bear to let you go.
Even if I don't marry you yet awhile
That don't mean that I mightn't change my mind.
What will I ever do without my chum?
Please don't go, Frank! Oh, please don't go and leave me! "

What could I do when Nellie talked that way?
Me, the poor fish I was! I passed it up.
I give that wonderful job up for her.
I says, " Nellie, of course I wouldn't leave you!
Maybe, some day; maybe you'll change your mind, —
About us marryin', I mean: I'll stay! "
And then I runs down to my boss's house,
And told him I was sorry, I couldn't go.
" Why? " says the boss. I couldn't tell him why.

He ramps and rages all around the joint,
And then he yells out, " I'll be good and damned!
I thought you was a salesman. You're a fool!
Well, I don't have no fools workin' for me.
You find yourself another job next Sadd'y! "

That very night I seen that bird, Ike Bloom,
That runs the Bee Hive, and he was so glad

To get me workin' there, he snapped me up,
And give me thirty-five per week — five more
Than I was gettin' from my reg'lar boss.

You should of saw how Nellie took the news.
She cried some more, and says, " Frank, I ain't worth it!
Frank, you're the finest thing in all the world! "
And then she kissed me. But it wasn't real, ,
The way it should of been. It wasn't real.

IV

I got along with Bloom, though not so well,
But still not so's I had a real kick comin'.
Nellie and me was better pals than ever;
And all the time I thought that I could see
That she was gettin' so she loved me right.
Then Fall come round, and Nellie went away
Down to Peoria, to see her sister.
She wrote to me three times in the first week,
And then, the second week she wrote me oncet,
And then I didn't hear another word
For ten days. Was I worried? Well, I ast you.
I was just goin' to take a train down there
And see what was the trouble, when the phone rang,
And it was Nellie, sayin' to come down
For supper, that she was so glad to hear me,
And wanted me to meet a friend of hers
That come up home with her.

                      I was mad and hurt,
And maybe didn't talk the way I should of.
At any rate, she says, " Please don't be mad;

63

I can explain it all when you come down."
Well, of course just by luck it had to happen
That Bloom and me was takin' inventory,
And so I had to go without the supper,
And didn't get to Nell's till after nine.
The first thing that I seen was a big guy —
Not a girl, like I thought — about six foot,
Big as a house, settin' there on the sofa;
I never seen a bird so much at home.
Nellie jumps up, and blushes, then she stutters,
" Frank! Why, I thought that you was never comin'.
My, I'm so glad to see you: meet Sam Finch —
Sam, this is Frank you heard me talk about.
I know that you and him will be good friends."

Now, how's that for a greetin' from your girl?
She kep' right on. " Sam's from Peoria,
And rode up with me. He's on business here.
Now ain't that nice? We're goin' to a movie.
Come on along." And all the time this goof,
This Finch, was actin' like I wasn't there,
And starin' at her, whiles she kept on blushin'.

I felt all sick inside, and says, " No, thanks,
I'm tired out. I'll see you later on."
She didn't beg me, like she wanted me,
And so I walked back home, wantin' to cry.

v

Next night, right after work, I goes to Nell's,
Just like the old days, without callin' up.

64

There was this Finch again. It made me sore.
I says, " Look here, Nell, are you busy now?
I'd like to see you." Nell looks round at Finch,
And hesitates, and says, " Well, Frank, you see — "
But that was all the further that she got.
Finch gets up to his feet and grabs his hat,
And turns around to Nell: " Now, listen, Nell.
Just get me right. Now, when I got a date
With you, I got it, see? Without no others
Around. Good-night! " and then he walks right out.
She jumps up from the chair and follows him.
And I can hear her beggin' him outside
Not to get sore. I waited five whole minutes,
Then I runs out the back door, and keeps runnin'.

Well, I got through my work next day, some how.
I was through feelin'. Somethin' way inside
Was dead, and that was all. I was quite cool,
And went to supper, et a little grub,
And walked into her parlor, without knockin'.

Part of a song kept singin' in my ear,
" Love 'em and leave 'em! Love 'em and leave 'em! " Right!
I grinned when I seen what I thought I'd see:
That big bum sittin' with her on the sofa.
He had his arm around her, and he kept it
Around her. He just gives a dirty look
At me, and hollers out, " No fish to-day! "

Nell gives a jump, but he just holds her there.
And all her jumpin' didn't make no difference.
For I sure knew that I had got the gate.

65

" Take her," I says, " You take her and be damned!
Nellie, I wanta thank you for a lesson.
Never again for me! Never again!
' Love 'em and leave 'em! ' That's me, from now on! "

I wonder where it could of went to. . . .
  I know I seen it just as plain:
A beautiful, big fairy city
  Shinin' through the rain.

Rain, it was, not snow — in winter!
  Special-order April weather
Ticklin' at our two faces
  Pressed up close together.

Not a single soul was near us
  Standin' out there on the bow;
When we passed another ferry
  He says, sudden, " Now! "

Then I looked where he was pointin'. . . .
  I seen a magic city rise. . . .
Gleamin' windows, like when fields is
  Full o' fireflies.

Towers and palaces in the clouds, like . . .
  Real as real, but nice and blurred.
" Oh . . ." I starts in — but he whispers,
  " Hush! Don't say a word!

" Don't look long, and don't ast questions;
  Elset you make the fairies sore. . . .

They won't let you even see it
   Never any more.

"Don't you try to ever go there. . . .
   It's to dream of, not to find.
Lovely things like that is always
   Mostly in your mind."

Somethin' made me say, "It's Jersey!" . . .
   Somethin' mean. . . . He hollers, "Hell!
Now you done it, sure as shootin'. . . .
   Now you bust the spell!"

Sure enough, the towers and castles
   Went like lightnin' outa sight. . . .
Nothin' there but filthy Jersey
   On a drizzly night.

Emotion Bourgeoise

You thought it was the Spring. The river crinkled
  Like creamy ribbon in the moon's incandescence.
  The stage was set: here was the very essence
Of middle-class romance: some far bell tinkled

And down a warm wind came a sudden flood
  Of lilac! Then you shuddered as my lips
  Brushed on your cheek, your hair, your finger-tips. . . .
And, "Don't!" you said, "I'm just not in the mood!"

You wrenched away, laughed a self-conscious titter,
  Spoke some banal something about the "Spring,"
  Entered the doorway with a little fling,
Leaving me somewhat flustered, somewhat bitter. . . .

Twenty! And May! (And several years ago. —
Hell! . . . That the scent of lilacs should hurt so! . . .)

I go back to the old house
  When the years have fled.
Blindfolded, I could walk
  With a sure tread
Queer little passageways,
  Quaint beloved halls,
Guided by the old feel
  Of well-loved walls.

I dodge from the huge chest
  That stood beside the stair.
I grope all about the hearth
  For the great chair;
And at the sacred small room
  None else could know
I claw at the secret door
  Locked long ago. . . .

And yet, to me, who loved you in that day,
(As still), " You do not understand," you say!

I have pursued Beauty
   All my life long —
Beauty, that sets the heart swelling
   In a sudden song. . . .

I have searched twilight woods,
   Seen Beauty's trace;
Watched reflected flames from Beauty
   Flash in a face.

Found Her spirit in a verse
   Fleetingly caught;
Viewed Her shadow, that some painter
   Lovingly wrought;

Felt Her strength stand in stone
   Almost unblurred;
Guessed the echo of Her voice
   In music I heard.

These I found — but Herself
   Slipped always past
Till one day I saw Her clear,
   Captured at last!

Rhythm of form, rhythm of soul —
Straightway I knew
I need never seek again —
Beauty was you!

" Here, kitty, kitty, kitty! " Such a cat!
Look at her, layin' there so fat and lazy,
With them big green eyes glued on Uncle Heinie.
She won't do nothin' without he says to do it,
And he won't say to, and she knows that, too;
So she's that spoilt!

            Oh, well, she's all he has
To love or care for. Nothin's left but her,
Exceptin' only me, and I don't count;
I don't get over only oncet a month,
It's so far, and so dirty all around,
And Uncle Heinie ain't no Cheerful Willie,
Just settin' there and never opens his face,
Stitchin' and stitchin'. . . . Gee, this yella gas,
Like it was sick to its stummick — I can't see.
My Fred won't never come; and Uncle Heinie
I know he hates it too; but he can't move,
" Too poor," he says. . . . And then, he hopes he'll die soon:
" Tired, so tired," that's all he ever says.
Look at him jab and jab with that there thread —
The poor old thing, I feel like it was a knife,
And he was jabbin' with it at my heart.
" Here, Uncle Heinie, let me thread it . . . so!
You oughta borry the eyes from that there cat —
She ain't no eighty years old. Here you be!

Go on and sew now. . . ."

                    Wonder what he does
For threadin', other times; just jabs, I s'pose,
Till by and by he hits it by mistake. . . .

He sets a lot and dreams about the farm,
The one he saved four thousand dollars for,
Over in Jersey. Cute little place it was,
A acre o' truckland, and a little cottage
That him and Cousin Erma was to live in.
Twelve years he scrimped and scraped the pennies up,
After his wife — that's Aunt Louisa — died.

This Cousin Erma was the only kid —
She wasn't no kid, o' course, more a old maid;
Maybe she coulda married, but I doubt it —
Her face was doughy-like, and she was skinny,
And never had no pep. Well, anyways,
You couldn't pry her loose from Uncle Heinie.
She useta help him in the tailor-shop here,
And cook, and carry the clo'es around, and all.
And him — to hear him talk about his Erma,
You woulda thought she was some Movie Queen.

I come down here the day that she was thirty.
There was those two, out settin' on the stoop,
Talkin' about the farm. " Five hundred dollars
Is all we gotta have before we go
And leave this dirty shop," he was just sayin',
" And we gets cabbages, and chickens, see?
And, Erma baby, maybe a little place
For flowers, huh? " and then he strokes her head.

I almost had to laugh, it was so comical,
Him callin' that old maid his " Erma baby,"
And maybe woulda. Only just that minute
She gives a cough like from down in her shoes.

He seen me jump, and give a little frown.
" She got a little cold a while ago;
It'll go 'way, I guess, now the Spring comes."
" A little cold! Good-night," I says to myself.
And while them two was fixin' up the supper
I goes around to old Doc Henderson.
He comes back with me, and he gives one look,
While she was coughin'. Then he looks her over,
And him and Uncle Heinie goes outside.

In a few minutes I hear Uncle Heinie
Out in the hall, cryin' and tryin' not to;
And then he creeps in, and his face looks green
Like he was drunk. And " So long farm," I thinks.

So long, is right. Gallopin' con it was.
Hospitals, and four months up to the mountains,
But nothin' helped. And finely the coffin
Chunkin' down outa sight. And every cent
Gone, and a couple hundred owed besides.

So back to all the sewin' and the pressin'.
Nothin' ahead but to get out of it —
First pay the bills, then live along some ways.
I wonder plenty times why he don't go
Down to the river and jump. But he just smiles
Sadlike, and works, and dreams about the farm,

I guess. I don't know if he's brave,
Or just too tired, or what. It doesn't matter.

So here he is, him and some lousy cat.
This'n's the third he has since Erma went,
I don't know if I should be shocked or not.
But — listen here — he calls them cats all " Erma."
Oh, well, I guess it reely ain't no harm,
Only — such awful cats.

        " What, Uncle Heinie?
You want the cat? Here, kitty, kitty, kitty!
Lord, such a cat! Here, Erma, Erma, Erma! . . ."

Dilemma

Gee, she's sweet! So sorta eyes wide open
   And shiny, like the street-lights do at night
When rain is on the sidewalk. They's a somethin'
   About the way her whole face has that light

Whenever she looks at me. It always says,
   " I believe in you! Oh, I believe in you! "
That face like a little flower, starin' at me —
   It scares me! What should I do? What *can* I do?

I tell her not to go and dream about me,
   I ain't no fine guy, and I tell her so;
She keeps on thinkin' I'm just kiddin' her,
   And answers back, "You can't fool me! I know! "

And just to think, that lovely dream about me
   Has got to smash all up some awful day
When she finds out the way that I am really. . . .
   It'll hurt her so. . . . I ought to get away

Where she can't never see me any more,
   Before that dream and all that sweetness dies. . . .
But can I do it? Can I do without her?
   Can I stand not seein' that lovin' in her eyes? . . .

Yeh, Miss Brown, that's the Parrot over there —
"Parrot," that's what the other boarders calls her.
You'll see what they mean before you been here long.
I always makes it a rule to tell new boarders
About that woman. My, she's such a fool!
Look at her. Every night for eight years, now,
She comes down dressed-up like a circus-horse,
With either that dress that's got the spangles on,
Or either a red thing like a ol' plush curtain.
Dolled-up to kill! And cheeks all painted young;
Tryin' to make you think she was somebody.

Somebody — her! Why, she ain't scarcely got
Money enough to pay for board and lodgin'.
I know her! Ain't I seen her, now, eight years,
And had to clean that attic room she has?

Miss Blodgett has a nawful time with her;
I wonder why she lets her stay at all.
I ast her oncet, and this is what she says,
" She useta be a reg'lar person, Martha.
And then, I'm sorta sorry for her, too."
Oh, that Miss Blodgett got the softest heart!

A reg'lar person! Well, that sure beats me.
Parrot, that's what. They make her set way down

78

Next to the Colonel, and he's awful deaf,
And all her screechin' don't make any difference.
I useta wait on table, and it made me
Right sick to hear the way she carried on:
" Aow, yess, the home we had at Narrergansett,
And twenty servants — aow yess! — twenty servants!
And aow, how well it all comes back to me,
The night we entertained for Pres'dent Cleveland —
He was a pers'nal frien' of my poor husban' " —
And all that sort of stuff. Oh, my, Miss Brown,
She just goes on and on and on that way.

Don't never let her get a-holt of you,
She'll talk your ear off.

                    All the other boarders,
They run away the minute they see her comin'.
It ain't no use to try to be nice to her,
No matter how lonely she is. Give her a inch,
She takes a couple miles. And such a bore!
So there she sets, playin' her solitary
With them ol' cards. I guess it was the truth
About her husban' havin' all that money,
But that was years ago. He lost it all
And dies right after. . . . And maybe it's the truth
All about Cleveland. . . . And she's kinda crazy
After all that, findin' things this way now.
But still, she is a fool, and that's a fac',
And people ain't goin' to stand for her, that's all.

Poor ol' Parrot. . . .
                    But Parrot, just the same. . . .

Why, Judge, I swear to God I wasn't soused!
What do I care what that there dumb cop says?
Why, sure, I'm fifty-three years old, but say,
What does that matter? . . . Judge, it's like I tell you:
There was them kids, yellin' and spinnin' tops,
And — just like that, before I even thinks,
I wants to spin one, too. I asts the kid,
He acks like I was nuts. And so I grabs one,
And winds the string, the way I useta do,
And throws it, and — it spins, I swear — it spins!
The kid is yowlin' — then this cop comes up —
My God, Judge — can't you understand? — it's Spring! . . .

Two Ways

Oncet in the Museum
  We seen a little rose
In a jar of alcohol —
  You turns up your nose:
" That's the way people think
  Love ought to be —
Last forever! Pickled roses!
  None o' that for me! "

That night was fireworks
  Out to Riverview —
Gold and red and purple
  Bustin' over you.
" Beautiful! " you says then,
  " That's how love should be!
Burn wild and die quick —
  That's the love for me! "

Now you're gone for good . . . say,
Wasn't they no other way? . . .

Settin' . . . and sewin' . . . and fixin' supper . . . and set-
 tin' . . .
And waitin' . . . and rockin' . . . and maybe they come
 home late,
And Elsie runs right out, when supper's over,
Every night it's the same, a dance or a movie,
And Fred goes out to the pool-room 'round the corner,
And Jim's too tired to talk, just reads the paper,
And then lays down and snores. . . . Well, I don't blame
 him;
At least he don't go wastin' it on licker,
And never did. He spends it on them kids,
And that's the most a man can do, at that,
When his wife dies, and all he has to help him
Is one ol', wore-out woman the kids calls " Gramma,"
And don't think knows a thing about what life is.

Well, I was that way oncet . . . they got to learn
The same as me, with awful knocks and kicks.
It sure don't do no good to try and tell 'em.
Of course, I wisht they'd set around and chat
About what's goin' on. . . . My, can't they see
That I ain't goin' to scold 'em? But they can't.
I hear 'em whisperin' every now and then,
"Dear ol' Gramma — she wouldn't understand."
And when they do talk, it's like to a baby.

So there it is . . . settin' and rockin' and sewin',
And cookin' supper, and settin' — that's what they think.

My! Don't I fool 'em! If they only knowed
The million things I'm doin' all the time!

All the ol' friends come back; they's Tom and Katie,
And all the ones when Frank and me first married;
And Frank, hisself, that never goes away
Even though I know he's dead for seven years,
Or — no — it's eight . . . what does it matter at all?
If only a grind-organ's playin' up the alley,
Or just a puff of wind blows through the window,
And smells like Spring, or anything else in the world,
Or the hot-potato man is yellin', " Po-ta-toes! " . . .
Or I look out and watch the little kids
Ridin' the penny-a-ride merry-go-round,
Why a whole string of things starts happenin':
And Jim ain't a widower with two kids to look after,
He's only my baby his self . . . or ain't even born yet. . . .

I can be any years old that I want to. . . .

It's all just like a merry-go-round, at that;
'Round and 'round and 'round; you never get far
From where you started in, no matter how fast
You think you're goin'. . . . Well, it don't do no good
To cry because the ride is slowin' down. . . .

" Pore ol' Gramma." . . . " She wouldn't understand." . . .
Settin', and rockin' . . . and fixin' supper . . . and set-
    tin'. . . .

Eat your cake, and have it, too —
That's you.
That's you, from the first day to the end:
" Won't you still be my friend? " —
Even though everything we useta have is like a busted bar-
rel —
" Have we got to quarrel?
I need you! They's a lot that you can give me yet! "

Yeh? Still tryin' to get what you can get,
And givin' nothin' back!
They's one thing I ought to give you: that's a crack
In the jaw. . . . Aw, what the Hell am I tryin' to say!
Why should I try and fool you, anyway?
As if you didn't know I druther die
Than ever hurt you. . . . Hell! What a silly lie!

Listen! Have you got any idear what you're astin' me?
Me, cut all to pieces with things that useta be. . . .
I wonder do you know
How they ain't but a couple places I can go
Without a somethin' chokin' my throat . . . that's only
part. . . .
I can't even hear some rotten tune
If they's anything in it about " June "
Without I think somebody's kickin' my heart. . . .

And, Oh My God! Just to see
You look and look at him, yeh, him — the very way
That only yesterday
You useta look at me! . . .
Oh well . . . you're you, and that's all there is to it.
Who could expect you could change? You couldn't do it.
Take everything, and give as little as you can.

What if I am a also-ran?
You love him, yeh? But you swear you need me still?
And I can't break away, and I don't suppose I never will.
I guess I'm a boob and a fish, . . . but who can tell? . . .
Oh, well. . . .

I'll go on bein' the one to talk to you,
And cheer you up when you get blue;
And when you want to talk, I'll understand
The same as always . . . " like nobody elset in the world "
        . . . and —

All right . . . what difference does it make?
I'll go on bein' . . . cake. . . .

I was hikin' along the road by Simmonsville.
I useta go out somewheres every Sunday
And walk off all the dirt and noise and nerves
That come from the week in the city in the store;
And say, it was like I made myself clean over.

I could see the top of the hill from where I was,
And I was gettin' excited the way I did
When I been trampin' up-hill for a ways
In some place where I never was before,
And played games with myself about the view
That's comin' when I hit the top: you know:
" Will it be a river twistin' through the woods,
Or a drop that makes your breath stick in your throat,
Or will it be only nothin', after all,
Exceptin', just the plain, everyday country? "
It's a great game, I'll say. . . . I useta love it.
And half the fun's not knowin' what is comin'. . . .
Well fifty yards, maybe, is still to go,
And I stops up to get my second wind,
And then that sign it slaps me in the eye:
" Picture Ahead! "

Can y' imagine it?
" Picture Ahead! " . . . I ast you! What the Hell!
Is that the fix that all of us has got to?

Is that what machinery was went and done?
Autos, and airryoplanes, and railroad trains,
And all the helps the papers yells about,
Tellin' us how the worl' is so much better,
And what a bunch of boobs our fathers was?
They want to make us all machines, is that it?
Even they got to take away the fun
Of guessin' what is comin' on the road!
They tell us, "Hurry! Get the camera out!
You ain't got sense enough to tell what's what.
You can't tell when they's anything worth seein'."

I got so mad, I went and jumped the fence,
And run acrost the field. Damned if I'd go
And see a sight that was all canned, you might say,
Or like a travel-movie. . . .

                    All my life
I had my fun pretendin' to myself
That every view I seen belonged to me,
Different from anybody's, mine especial.
"Picture Ahead!"

                    I stopped there in the field,
And turned aroun', and beat it for the train.

I just can't get the heart to go no more.
The country's spoilt, and lots of things is spoilt,
Just on account that sign. . . . I feel so old,
And everything I see looks old and worn-out.

Machinery! . . . Machinery! . . . "Picture Ahead!" . . .

The Sowing

(Fort Sheridan — Spring, 1917)

Placid breezes sauntering
  Over a lake of glass,
Kissing the pouting elm-buds,
  Patting the new grass;
Turquoise overhead
  Swimming May skies —
("Trench-knives are top-hole
  For gouging out their eyes.")

Great bees, clover-laden,
  Solemnly drone past;
All the glad world shouts
  Of Spring come at last.
Bobolinks, meadowlarks
  Bursting with May —
("If you can't pull the bayonet out,
  Shoot the body away!")

Maggie and me was standin' at the gate
At Luna, and I was lookin' through the purse,
And couldn't seem to find the change I needed;
Just then I heard a sorta nice soft voice,
"Please, won't you let us take you in? You must!"

I looks up quick, thinkin', "Gee, here's some flat-hat"
(Flat-hat's a college-willy) "tryin' to make me."
I was just goin' to tell him where to get off,
And then I seen that smile — and what could I do?

He *was* a flat-hat, too, and one them collars,
Soft, and they button down, and a herring-bone
Suit like the reg'lar flat-hats always wears;
The hat was in his hand, and he was bowin',
So sorta shy, and that there curly smile!

His friend was edgin' over towards Mag,
Even scareder, and dumb; I never did see him plain
All evenin'; I was lookin' at that smile
The boy that talked to me had. The hard words
Stopped, and there I am, smilin' right back,
And then I hear myself sayin', " All right."

There ain't a thing in Coney we didn't do.
And all the while Jack was so awful sweet,

Actin' like Mag and me was high-brow ladies,
And tellin' me what a good sport I was.

The more I watched that curly smile he had,
The more I started to get crazy about him.
And still he stayed polite. We went in shows,
And won a Kewpie on the Wheel of Chance,
And say! They sure spent money! Then we went
Down to the Steeple-chase, and all dressed up
Like clowns, and bumped the bumps, actin' like nuts.
We didn't miss a trick. Did we get fun!

Ten o'clock come, and we took off the clown rig,
And had a sanwich and a couple sodas,
And danced. I never thought nobody ever
Could dance the way that darlin' Jack could dance.
None of that jazzin', none of that cheek to cheek,
Just like goin' to sleep, and dreamin' dreams
Where music was part. He didn't hardly touch me,
But just his fingers felt like they was red-hot,
And burnt me. . . . That's the way he made me feel,
I was so wild about him by that time.

But him, he just stayed smilin', and polite,
And scared, and called me a " good sport " again.

The dancin' stopped. I seen the big moon shinin',
And says, " Come on, let's ditch them other two
Just for a minute. There's the Dip of Death!
I want to ride! Come on! " . . . So he says, " Sure."

You see, I took that ride plenty of times;
And first it scares you green, then they's a tunnel

That lasts about a minute. If I could only
Get him in there, where nobody could see us,
Maybe I'd make him quit that bein' polite;
Maybe he might forget that " good sport " stuff,
Maybe he'd put his arm around me, maybe
He'd hug me so it hurt — that would be beautiful,
To have him hurt me — oh, that curly smile! —
The way I felt, I woulda been glad to die
That minute, if he'd only kiss me oncet
And mean it . . . he was so scared . . . and young . . .
    and clean. . . .

I didn't screech a bit goin' down the dip,
And when we got to where the tunnel started,
My heart was chokin' up against my teeth.
He sat there smilin', half a inch away.
Listen. You know I'm pretty. Yes, I am.
I can have any boy I want to, can't I?
Can y' imagine how it made me feel
To be so crazy about that darlin' Jack,
And have him ack like he didn't want to touch me?
I couldn't stand it for a second longer.
" Jackie! " I wispers, " Jackie! " Then I takes
His face in both hands, presses my lips
Against his. . . .

            And he kissed me! It was like
I wasn't anybody any more,
But meltin', meltin' away. . . .

            One kiss, that's all.
But when I'm old and lame and shriveled up,
I bet I'll feel that kiss still burnin' me!

We didn't ride again. We walks back quiet,
Not sayin' nothin'. I couldn't of, anyways.
Then Jack says, quick, " I'm 'fraid we'll have to go.
I got to take the mid-night home to Cleveland."

Cleveland! And never see him any more?
Never again? What is he tryin' to say?
" Gee, Florrie, but you sure are one good — "

                                        " Jack! "

I says, sudden. Everything in the world,
It seemed to me, was in that curly smile.
I pulls him to one side, and wispers to him.

Oh, yes, I did. I ain't a bit ashamed!
He hangs his head, and turns all red and pink,
And stutters, " No, I'm sorry, I got to go.
Good-night, and thanks a lot." Then they both leaves,
Not lookin' 'round at all. I watched 'em go,
And then the tears come, and I couldn't stop.
Mag got sore at me cryin', and we scrapped,
And don't speak now.

                        But what is Mag to me?
You know me, and you know how proud I am.
You know there ain't no boy can ever say
That I would let him do more than just kiss me,
And honest to God, I never kissed one back.
They say I'm cold, and not no fun at all.
Well, let 'em talk. . . . All I can see at night
Before I go to sleep, or in the daytime,
Measurin' goods, is that there curly smile! . . .

I wisht to Heaven them college-boys would quit
Wearin' them flat-hats! Oh, it's like a knife
Was cuttin' me, just to see hats like them.
Never see him again . . . not even know
What his address is . . . and that curly smile. . . .
" A good sport " . . . oh, his mouth . . . flat-hats . . . oh
    well. . . .

Yes sir, it is a big crowd for a funeral;
The biggest I seen in all the seven years
That I been George's helper, he's the sexton.
No sir, it ain't no famous man at all.
It's just a funny-lookin' little old maid,
That everybody useta call " The Crank,"
And laugh at, and get sore at, both together.
But here they all are, comin' to her funeral.

Oh, My! I guess they wasn't anything
Around this church she didn't stick that long,
Skinny old nose in. If it was plantin' trees,
Or washin' pews, or puttin' 'round the hymn-books,
Or anybody's job at all, she'd come
Buttin' in everywhere, tellin' us how to do it.
By Jiminy, I bet it's more than oncet
I heard her tellin' the Rector how to preach!

Well, it was just she was a born school-teacher.
I don't suppose no man ever wanted to kiss her;
Gee, such a lemon-face! And so I guess
Not ever havin' a husband to boss around,
Or give her a wallop oncet awhile his self,
She took it out in makin' the school-kids hop.
Her classes always was the best in school,
Scared of her, but you bet your neck they studied.

And us — well, when she said a thing, we jumped;
And, tell you the truth, the reason why this church
Is the fine important place it is right now,
Is all of half because of old Miss Jobson,
The way she useta get things all stirred up.

She was the kind that always ast for work;
You couldn't pile enough on to her shoulders,
Pore little slantin' things. And every year
The Xmastide Bazaar was her big time.
That's when they let her loose; and man, she went it!

Well, just a year ago, she had a cold,
And there was all that big Bazaar to run,
And all three of the ladies that useta help her
Was moved away. The Rector goes and asts her
Whether she shouldn't oughta give it over
To some of the men to do? She flew right up,
And coughin' like she was, she took his head off:
They wasn't nobody goin' to run her job.
And she dives in, and for three mortal weeks
She does a dozen people's work herself.
And what I mean, we had the best Bazaar
This church is ever had, or any other.
Three times the reg'lar fund that goes to the Homeless!
And the night it was finished, Miss Jobson goes to bed.

March come, and the pore old thing was still in bed;
And then the summer, and she laid there still;
And now . . . here is the crowd that's at her funeral.

Mister, I says it now, there was some woman!
Cranky, and buttin'-in, and sour-faced —

95

But lemme tell you, if they is a Heaven,
And I get there some day, I know one thing:
The first sight that I'll see 'll be Miss Jobson,
Orderin' angels round, and tellin' the Lord
His self what he should do. . . . Some woman, mister!

I found a scar across my wrist to-day.
  I got it gathering apple-blossoms for you
  One breathless afternoon when Spring was new,
And all the trees were wearing white, for May.

I had forgotten any scar was there —
  I had forgotten, too, the trifling pain
  Quite paid-for with a kiss . . . and then, the rain
Scattering transient diamonds in your hair. . . .

You thought you loved me then, do you remember?
  And I, for my part, poured out, I am sure,
  Brave words like " grow," and " strengthen," and " en-
    dure." . . .
But that, of course, was May — this is November.

Time will be-dim that night . . . the blooms . . . your
    face . . .
Even the scar will heal to a faint trace. . . .

✻ MORE "IN AMERICAN" ✻

So Pa yells out, " Why ain't the dinner done yet? "
And Ma says, " They was a fire down the block,
And fourteen fire-engines. It was excitin'! "
And Pa yells louder, " Oh, for the love of God!
Ain't you got nothin' to do but be a leaner?
That's what the whole bunch of you are — just leaners."
He said a whole lot more, and so did Ma.
He's always naggin' her about bein' a leaner.

But Ma and me don't care. In the afternoons
We get a pillow apiece, and rest it down
On the window, and Ma puts her arm around me,
And we can see everything, like a reg'lar movie.
The L trains whizzin' by, chuck full of people,
And I wave, and they wave back to me again.
And the day the dog bit Frankie, across the street
I seen it, and it was awful. And Mr. Blake
Come along another time and hit Miz Blake,
And fell down in a mud-puddle. And the scissors-man
Comes by, and the rags-a-lion, and the grind-organ,
And a wop funeral, with a great big band;
And Ma says, " Did you see Miz Glibbick, Edna?
She's havin' chicken tonight. Look in the basket."
And one time when I got the pillow fixed,
There was that stuck-up Johnny Wade, that's only
Just fifteen, and he thinks he's awful smart

Because he got long pants. And there he was
Right underneath the window, with that girl
That just moved in at the corner. And he kissed her,
And I told Ma, and I ran and got a glass
Of water, and threw it on 'em. And was he mad!
And yestiddy, a poor old horse fell down,
And it took all afternoon to get him up —

What do we care if Pa does call us " leaners " ?

One day Ma come home
    And says, " Look what I got! "
And it was a little plant
    In a round pot.
Then she put it in the window
    And says, " Watch it grow.
It'll have a pretty flower
    First thing you know."

So all the time, weeks and weeks
    I kept waterin' it.
The wall next door was very high.
    It hardly got a bit
Of sunshine. It was dark
    All day. And at night
I thought it was kept awake
    By the arc-light.

It wouldn't bloom; and it never
    Growed worth a cent.
I think it was a silly plant,
    Because it got all bent
Stretchin' towards that arc-light
    Like it was tied. . . .
When I told her what I thought,
    Ma cried.

When I'm all through, and you got to get rid of me,
Don't go shootin' the bunk, or makin' prayers,
And all that stuff. And don't go stickin' me
Into no stuffy cemetery lot.
I want some room . . . I got to have room . . . I got to!

So if you really want to take the trouble,
You take what's left, and put it in a fire,
The hottest you can find — and let 'er burn!
Till I ain't only a handful of grey somethin'.
" Ashes to ashes " — ain't that a whole lot cleaner
Than " dust to dust "? You let old fire have me.

Then you just cut them ashes in four parts.
Take the first ashes to the side of a mountain,
Heave 'em up to the wind . . . I used to love
The way it's quiet and strong and big up there.

The second ashes, take 'em down to the ocean;
And when the waves come pilin' up the beach,
Scatter 'em where the green starts to get foamy.
They used to sing me songs about havin' nerve,
And never gettin' tired, or givin' in —
Let 'em run, and take me with 'em.

And the third part, you go out to the country,
Into some wide, long field, and spread 'em round.

Maybe they'll help the grass to climb a little.
I can remember how I used to roll,
And dig my face down in, and sniff and bite it,
And lay back on it, just a crazy kid,
And watch the clouds go skippin' over the sky,
And the bees, and the crazy birds, and everything
Would get so perfect I would want to cry.

Then they'll be one part left. You take that down
Where's they's the thickest crowds, right in the city.
And when nobody's lookin', give it a sling
Onto the sidewalk, underneath their feet.
The pore things, always hoofin' it along,
Somewheres, they don't know where, and I don't either.
Always lookin' for somethin' — wonder what?
I never got very near 'em. A person can't,
Even when you want to. Everybody's scared,
So scared, you know . . . so scared! But a bunch of ashes
Maybe might get real close to somebody once.

Just once. . . .

" Well, boys, how would you like to go to the circus? "
Say, maybe Ern and me didn't jump up!
I'm goin' on ten, and Ern is most eleven,
And neither of us hadn't saw a circus.

" Yessir, it's Treeman's great big three ring circus,
Lions, and taggers, and elephants, and all.
I got a couple tickets for two smart boys."
Ern drops his fishin' pole. " Oh, gee," he says,
What do we have to do? " The little man
Gets down outa the buggy and blinks through his glasses.
" Well, now, you see, this circus changed the route;
They're comin' to your town, and here I got
A lot of posters yet that ain't been posted.
Now what I want, you tell me where to find
The man that owns that barn." I looks around.
" What barn? " I says. " Why, that there one," he says.
And then he points his finger at the schoolhouse!
Say, maybe he was only tryin' to fool us,
Or maybe his eyes was reely awful bad.
Or else he didn't care, so long as he
Could get his posters up, and blame somebody.
At any rate, I starts to say, " That ain't — "
But like a flash, Ern kicks me in the shin,
And says, " That barn? What that barn ain't nobody's.
You can put all the posters there you want to."

The man, he looks at Ern a couple seconds,
And then says, " Fine! " and starts goin' over to it.

Then Ern, he whispers to me, " Don't be silly!
It's such a grand big joke on that old Mears!
The darn old meanie, tellin' Pa about
Us gettin' F, in deportment. And besides,
You don't think Pa would get us any tickets.
Come on and help! We got to see that circus! "

" But s'posen we get caught? " Aw, don't be silly! "
Says Ern, " He's just a blind old foolish thing!
Anybody that can't see it's a schoolhouse —
How's he ever goin' to tell that it was us? "

" Come on, here, boys," the poster-man was sayin',
" Come on and earn your tickets." So we went.
And gee, the way we stuck them posters up!
The animals, and a lady on a horse,
And a Loop-the-loop, with monkeys on bicycles,
And the grandest lot of things you ever saw!
In just a minute or so, the place was covered!

And then the man gave us our tickets, and left,
And we just rolled around the ground and laughed
About the joke that we was goin' to have,
And all about how mad old Mears would be!

So then, we went on home, but all the time,
I kept on worryin' about bein' caught
And what would happen then. But Ern just laughed,
And says, " Of all the scaredy-cats! Oh, gee! "
But just the same, I didn't feel easy, nossir.

Nobody didn't seem to think of us.
They was an awful row about the posters,
And Mears was just so mad he couldn't spit,
And the circus people had a lot of trouble,
But they fixed that all right, and Thursday come,
And Friday, and tomorrow would be the circus,
And still nobody hadn't touched the posters;
And nobody hadn't ast us any questions.

It was too easy. Things don't go like that.

II

But anyways, Sa'ddy we done the chores,
And we was fixin' to slip off after dinner,
And Pa stopped all of a sudden talkin' to Ma
About tent-catapillas, and he says,
" Now, just a minute, boys! " and looks at us.
And doesn't say a word, just looks and frowns.
Oh, gee, I knowed that we was in for it!

Then Pa takes somethin' out of his back-pocket.
He opens his hand, and holds it under my eyes.
It was fishin'-line, but wrapped around some paper.
Doggone it, what did I wrap that line around
A Bible-card, with my name right on it, for?
" I guess you know who that belongs to, eh?
Old Mears, he picked that up off of the ground
Under the posters, early Wednesday mornin'.
That's all I have to say, ain't it? "

  Gee whiz!
That's Pa all over. Deep, he is, and quiet.

Just think of knowin' all week long, and never
Lettin' us guess he knew a thing about it!

"All right," he says, "you march along with me.
I got a little circus that you're goin' to."
He wasn't smilin' any. He was mad.
We was too scared to ast a single question.
Pa kept us a couple yards in front of him,
And pretty soon we got down to the schoolhouse.
He sets down on the steps, and lights his pipe
And takes out a "Breeder's Gazette," and a little book
And then he looks at all the posters there,
And says to us, "Well, boys, it's purty, ain't it.
The joke that you boys had was mighty funny.
Now, I got to have my little joke, myself.
Get out your pocket-knives. You're goin' to tear
All of them posters off, and what won't tear
You're goin' to scrape. We don't leave here tonight
Till every inch is off. Get busy, now,
So I can start in laughin'."

Oh, Gee whiz!
It kept on gettin' hotter all afternoon,
And we just tore and scraped, and scraped and tore.
Pa kept his eye right on us. If we stopped
To catch a breath, he'd start in: "All right, Ern.
Get back to work. Here, Jack, get busy, there.
It's such a joke I wouldn't want that you
Should miss a bit." My back begun to ache,
And both my hands got cramped. But you know Pa —
Once he gets a notion into his head —
And all the time the circus was goin' on!

109

We just kept thinkin' about the other boys.
That would be laughin' and hollerin'. And us two,
That was too far away even to hear
The band, because the circus was way away
Over the other side of town, on the edge.
Not even hearin' the band! That might of helped.

When we got half of the pictures, maybe, off,
I just couldn't stand bein' tired another second.
I didn't care if Pa whaled me. I laid down,
And I guess maybe I did cry a little.
Then Pa looks up from his book, and says, " All right.
Ten minutes off for rest." So Ern come over,
And whispers, " Oh, gee, Jack, I'm awful sorry! "
What good did that do? Why, right that minute we knew
The lady would be hangin' by her teeth
From the center-pole. . . . And all the big old elephants
Would be paradin', and bicycles loopin' the loop!
That made me start in cryin' all over again.

Pa seen me, and he stands up, and he stretches.
" Time's up," he says. " Sorry it makes you cry;
But you ought to thought of that before you done it.
Now. See that piece with all the monkeys on it?
You scrape awhile on that. Maybe it'll help you
Remember to cut out monkey-business hereafter."
He thought that joke was swell, and kept on chucklin'.

That's the way it went the whole afternoon.
Ern and me workin', and Pa settin' and readin',
And all the while us thinkin' about the circus.
The last part I was tired, it was just like

The time I had the measles and the fever.
And when ma hollered " Supper! " from the house,
I didn't even have enough sense to notice.

All through supper, Pa didn't talk to us.
We didn't care. Gee what a wonderful supper!
I et three helpin's of chicken and potatoes,
And green-apple pie! — two pieces! And six doughnuts!
Wasn't Ma grand to do that for us? Gee!
If we could only of got Ma to talk
To Pa in the first place — still she's sort of scared
The way we are. 'Cause lots of times she said,
" Your Pa's a just man, boys." That's a swell word, " Just! "

Ern and me was plumb stuffed full of supper.
I couldn't hardly walk. Ern, he set there,
And Ma comes over and gives us both a hug,
And kissed us; but Pa got up like he didn't see.
" Poor boys! " says Ma, " But don't you worry no more.
Your Pa is goin' to have Jed Allen come
And do the rest of the scrapin', and paint the school
Again. It's goin' to cost him fifteen dollars.
But I guess you learnt your lesson, didn't you? "

She kissed us again, and went into the kitchen.
Ern started cryin' this time. He was awful sleepy.
" I'm goin' up to bed," he says, and gulps.
The sun was still shinin', but we was ready for bed.
Ern went on up. But I listened at the door
To the kitchen, and heard Ma sayin' to Pa " Oh, my!
I feel so sorry for 'em. They got the tickets.
Why don't you let 'em go tonight? "

Pa snorted.
" Go ? Why say — they'd fall to sleep in their seats!
The place for them is bed. And besides which,
They got to have their lesson all complete."

Then Ma says, " Well — why don't you let 'em go Monday
To Olean ? Why — I could take 'em myself! "

But Pa got sort of mad, then. " No, I told you! "
He says real loud, " Olean ? Twenty miles!
Sue's feet is bad. No, not one step. Now drop it!
They's goin' to be other circuses other years."

Then Ma says, sort of to herself, " Yes, Frank.
I understand it better than you do.
No other circuses won't be like this one."

" Can't help it! " Pa yells, " That's the end of it! "
And he starts comin' over towards the door,
So I run quick upstairs, and gets to bed.

But I was thinkin' awful fast, you bet.
Olean, that's the place, that's what Ma said.
They ain't no way to get there but two roads.
One of 'em runs along in front of our house,
The other one is most a mile away,
Across our farm, and the hollow, and Brandt's farm.
Gee whiz! If we could only see the wagons! —
Ern, he was sleepin' with his clo'es still on.
I took mine off as quick as you can say it,
And pushed Ern over, and started shakin' him.
Then he woke up, and I begun to tell him.

Was he excited! " But how're we goin' to wake up?
We can't stay up all night, bein' so sleepy.
And they'll go awful early. That's the way
Circuses always do."

So then I says
" We can both go to sleep thinkin' about it.
And that way we'll wake up. Don't you remember
The way it worked last Fourth? "

So Ern says " Sure,"
And off we went to sleep. But both of us
Kept wakin' up, all night. It didn't do
Much good to go to sleep, anyways, 'cause
I just kept seein' cages and elephants,
And wagons, whirlin' round and round and round.

III

But after a while I heard a rooster crow,
And then another one. I jumped up quick,
And pulled up Ern, and ran to the east window.
Gee, was it still, and black as the inside
Of a black cat. But there was the roosters crowin',
And we thought the sun ought to be comin' up
Any time now. And it wasn't very cold,
'Cause it was the middle of June. Well, maybe I
Was scared. I wanted to go back to bed.
But Ern says " No! We just can't miss this much!
We just got to see it, and we got to go
Right now." So then we put our clo'es on quick,
And I quit shiverin', and we both took blankets,
To sit on, and we carried our shoes, and started.

Gee, was it scarey, goin' down the steps!
The boards kept creakin', and I didn't see
How Pa could stay asleep. I was just sure
That any second he would come a-runnin',
And give us Ned, and chase us back to bed.
But we got through the door, and into the yard.

It was so quiet we didn't dast to breathe
Out loud, and even the roosters had quit crowin'.
They wasn't a sound, and we couldn't see a thing.
But we ran down the road, away from the house,
And Ern comes over and whispers, " Say, you silly,
What makes you think this here's the road they'll take?
The other road's a whole lot better travellin'! "

Well, I just had a hunch they'd take the one
In front of our house. But of course, it's true
Brandt's road was lots the best. What could we do?

" I know," I says, " I'll stay here by this road,
And you go over by Brandt's, and watch, and so
Whichever way it comes, they's one of us
Will see it. If it's me, I'll run and find you,
And if it's you, you come and tell me. See? "

" Yeh, that's a swell idear," says Ern. " You think
I'm goin' way over there, acrost the holler,
With snakes and everything, and pretty near
A mile away? All by myself? No sir!
Why don't you do it yourself, if you're so smart? "
" Well, then," I says, " we got to both stay here.
You're the one thinks they're comin' the other road."

"They are! They are!" he says. "But just the same
We got to use some sense. Now just suppose
It comes there, how can I get back and tell you?
The both of us would miss it, doin' that.
You're such a dumb-head!"

Then I got the scheme.
"All right. I tell you. We'll get in the middle,
Right on the edge of the holler. And you watch
One road, and I'll keep watchin' on the other.
Then we can both run to the road it comes."

So that was what we did. Ern takes a blanket,
And goes to Brandt's side of the holler, and sets,
And I set on a little hill, on our side.

It was still awful black. I was so scared
I started to shiver again. And then a owl
Begun to hoot, and I knew all the time
It was a owl, but it scared me just the same.
And a fog commenced to come up from the holler,
And it looked just like a sheet you spread to dry.

Well, I set there, and started in to whistle,
And I listened, and told stories to myself,
About the lions and taggers, and I couldn't
See anything, or hear, and still the sun
Just wouldn't come up. And I was afraid
The fog would get so thick we couldn't see
The wagons when they come, and I was gettin'
So sleepy, and my eyes begun to hurt,
And I just laid on the blanket for a second. . . .

IV

All of a sudden Ern was shakin' me,
It was broad daylight, and the fog was gone.
And Ern kept yellin', over and over, " We missed it!
What did you have to go and go to sleep for!
We missed it! Why, it must of went long ago! "

We started runnin' back over to our place,
And I says, " Well, what're you yellin' about?
You went to sleep, too, didn't you? So, you see! "

We kept on runnin' over past the cow-shed,
And heard Pa milkin', but we didn't stop.
And in the road, we seen it, sure enough.
There was the tracks, some deep, deep tracks, and ruts
That didn't look more than an hour old.
And then we both just laid down on the grass,
And cried, and cried.

But after a minute or so,
I heard somebody behind us. It was Ma,
And she says, " Hello, boys! You up so early? "

Ern ran to Ma, and put his head in her apron.
And cried, and kept on sayin' " Ma! We missed it!
We didn't even get to see the wagons! "
Ma brought him over where I was, and hugged us,
And then says, " Look! Why, just look in the road! "

Then all three of us looked down in the mud,
At the side of the road, and there was a great big hole
As big as a barrel!

" Sure as you're born," says Ma,
" That's where the elephant stepped! " And we stopped
    cryin',
Because it was! It was round on the edges,
That was the place his toes was. Oh, gee whiz!
It was a great big elephant, I bet you!
We took the blankets, and some sticks, and made
A tent, and left a little hole, to peek through.
Ma didn't tell Pa about us gettin' up,
Or missin' the wagons — I mean, I guess she didn't,
He didn't say a word to us about it.

Then we went in, and had a great big breakfast,
And we was all excited, and I don't see
Why Ma kept wipin' her eyes, or why she said,
" Poor boys! I know a lot of folks that miss
Their circus in the fog."

We didn't miss it,
Not all of it. Because didn't we fix
A sign that said, " The Real Live Elephant's Foot,"
And charge a penny a look, and a whole crowd
Of the boys and girls came over, and paid a penny,
Even the ones that went to the reg'lar circus?

And then, maybe next year this time —
                                        Gee whiz!

I saw him once: a slender, tottering man
Stood on a stage; and seemed about to fall
At every moment; and a voice began,
Like a thin echo from some far-off wall,
To tremble through the room; and what it said
Concerned " the Arts " and " tireless endeavor " —
How heavy-handed years may bow the head,
But Beauty lifts the soul of man forever.
His hearers, smug in manner and attire
Of cosmopolitan sophistication;
That crumpled figure, lit as by a fire
With an unfashionable consecration —
Oh, futile gesture, fleeting as a breath!
Oh, Beauty, laughing in the face of Death!

I was steppin' along, whistlin',
  And Spring was liftin' my feet.
The buildings was all bright in the sun,
  There was gold in the street.

And just that minute, in the Square
  What did I have to see
Inside of a rusty wire cage
  But a scraggly tree.

" Help! Help! " I thought it said. . . .
  Its branches was all tired and thin. . . .
Was the cage to pertect it, and keep things out,
  Or the tree in?

Oh, I know it was silly, but right then
  My feet felt somethin' holdin' 'em down.
And the whistle was gone, and the gold was only
  A sick brown.

I

Dreams?
  Take 'em away!
Dreams?
  Never again for me!
Be good? — What does it get you?
Be true? — What to?
Real love? — Try and get it!
Success? — You can have it!

White shadows!
White shadows on green trees;
Green leaves, thick like a wall;
Green, so dark it's black;
Not a sound; nothin' movin';
Nobody knows;
Nobody cares —

Every time I close my eyes —
And I'm closin' my eyes most of the time,
But not to dream! —
If I could only get there, to them South Sea Islands!
Maybe I got a wrong idea about 'em,
Maybe I couldn't find what I want if I got there,
Maybe it's all the same if I go to Hell here or anywheres
    elst —

But I wisht to Heaven I never seen them books,
I wisht to Heaven I never heard of South Sea Islands,
   Or dances, or men,
   Or nothin' —

I always had two things different from most girls —
I was pretty, and I could shake the feet.
Night after night, down in Skaneateles,
I would lay in bed, with my eyes closed tight.
Sleep wouldn't come, only sorta dreams —
Ditchin' the store on Genesee Street,
Goin' to New York, gettin' on the stage,
Workin' to the top, name in lights —
I was pretty, and I could shake the feet.

All the time
There was that other dream —
Some man — a real man —
That I was goin' to love,
Some man that would be
Good enough for me,
But me too good for him —
See what I mean?
Gee, it's hard to say!
That would be love —
A real, real love —
Me lovin' him,
But him lovin' more!

But could I find that
In Skaneateles,
Say it with oil-cans!

Do I have to tell you about makin' the break?
And landin' a job, and three years in the chorus,
One in New York, and two on the road?
Three rotten years!
And then — the front row!

II

So then, six weeks ago, we started rehearsin'
For this " You Tell 'em " . . . I was livin' with Mame
On Seventy-second Street. And that first day,
Just as I was comin' out of the door
It was like somebody shot me in the chest.
Of course, nobody didn't really shoot me,
But there was a man, holdin' the door open.
You see? You understand? There was my dream!
Holdin' the door! I never seen him before,
But right away I knew that it was him.

I couldn't say a thing, exceptin' " Thank you! "
But all the way to the theater, a crazy song
Without no tune kept racin' round inside
My head: " He lives there, too! He lives there, too! "
I looked in the lookin'-glass by the stage door —
I didn't know myself, I was so pretty!

I gets into my place, and Mr. Long —
That's the director — give me just one look,
And goes to the corner, and whispers to the backer,
And says, " Miss Lane! Just step out here a second! "
The two of them, they give me the once-over,
And whispers, and then they put it up to me:

"Do you want to do a number by yourself?
A South Sea dance. I wouldn't be surprised
Was you the very girl we're lookin' for."

Well, what did I care for the dirty looks
The other girls was givin'? I started thinkin'
About that dream-man, that had held the door,
And I says to myself, "Good Luck! Already!"
They give me the dance, and five whole lines to say!
Was I excited! Ast me!

But what I was most excited about was the man.
It was a week till I could get Miss Rogers
She runs the boardin'-house — to interdooce us.
And then, the dumb way that I acted! My!
He was dumb-actin' too. And so up-stage!
Just about twenty-four is what he was,
But young for that; and he was sort of scared.
And I kept thinkin' he didn't have no use
For chorus-girls; thought he was too good for 'em,
I guess. Miss Rogers told me that he came
From a real good family out there in Cleveland,
And she heard he used to be engaged to a swell
That gave him the gate. That was three years ago,
And he was off of any kind of girls.

He told me somethin' about that, later on.
But that first night, all he managed to tell me
Was that he was in New York studyin' law,
And had to go up now and get to work.

He sorter squirmed, and kept on lookin' around,
And tryin' to get way. I was so mad!

I loved his curly hair, and his black eyes,
And the way he was so strong, and still so shy
And proud. Just a kid, really, and I wanted
To take his head and pull it down, and pat it,
And smooth his hair, and, you know, say, " There, there."

III

So a whole month went on, and I couldn't seem
To make a bit of progress with that boy.
'Cause every time I tried out some new gag,
Like bein' sympathetic, or actin' like
A two-year-old, hopin' I wouldn't scare him,
Or make that darn proud look come into his eyes,
It didn't get me much of anywheres.

The one time that he really opened up
Was just a little somethin' about the girl,
And how he hated her now, and he was glad
She threw him down, and taught him what girls was.

I says, " But women isn't all alike, Jack."
Then he froze up, and says, " Ain't they, Miss Lane ? "
Lettin' me know the " Jack "-stuff didn't get by.
Just think of that! The man I'd always dreamed of —
And when I found him, all he done was run!
I couldn't see why, 'cause Mr. Long kept sayin'
I had refine beauty, and was a ringer
For Elsie Ferguson, if you know what I mean.

But what could I do ? I bet I cried a bucket-full
A night. And when I didn't cry — I read!

Yeh, can you tie it? The readin' was Long's doin'.
It was when we started rehearsin' for the dance.
Long says to me, " Now, girlie, about this dance:
You sure do shake your dogs the way you oughta,
And, what I mean, you got the neck and shoulders,
And other things, includin' one cute face.
Now what you got to get is atmosphere.
Look. Here's a book about them South Sea Islands.
You take and read it. Don't you skip a page.
And when you get through this, I got two more."

Of course, I hated to start in on readin' it
But in three pages I couldn't leave it loose.
Readin' about them heathen, lovely places,
It was like fallin' into a different world.
Layin' in the sand, and watchin' big blue waves,
And nothin' to think of exceptin' love —
Love, and white shadows, and a round white moon.

Talk about atmosphere! I got so while
I was rehearsin' my dance, I would be thinkin'
About the things in the book. And just like magic
Those wasn't footlights there in front of me —
They was big sea-shells, on a lonely island.
And all the time I kept seein' Jack right there —
Jack, and his curly hair, and his black, black eyes.

And did I dance! All of a sudden I knew
That I was good. Long come right up, one day,
And he had a look he hadn't had before.
He takes my hand, and drags me to one side,
" Say, Janie Lane, you sure have got the stuff!

We certainly got some dancin' South Sea Kid!
But that ain't all I got to say. Look here,
I'm crazy about you, kid, and that's a fact.
What do you say you come and have dinner with me?"

It wouldn't have took no three-year-old to know
What he was drivin' at. And let me tell you,
He's some good-lookin' guy. And besides which
He sure has got some drag in the perfession.
But even while I was thinkin' all those things,
Jack and his eyes come poppin' in my mind,
And I answers up, "Why, Mr. Long! You know
You got a wife. I ain't that kind of a girl."

Long, he just smiles a sort of sad-like smile,
And says, "Well, if you know that much about me,
You know how much I care about the wife,
Or her about me, either. Don't you see?
I'm crazy about you, honey. If you want
To be my friend, I'll put you up among 'em.
I know the stuff you got. And if you'll let me
I'll make you the best dancin'-act on Broadway."

But I looked away. And he coughed a couple of times,
And then he says, "It's all right, Janie, dear.
Don't let it worry you. You just keep up
The good work. See? And if you think that you
Could ever love me — why, I'm right here, kid,
And always waitin' for you. See? Good-night."

Well, that was swell of him, wasn't it, now?
But I was wild about that Jack, of course,
And the Prince of Wales couldn't of made no impression.

And so it got to the day of the dress-rehearsal,
And Mame and me was comin' into the house;
Who should we see but Jack, with two big law-books.
Here was my chance. "Why Jack!" I starts right in,
"You're just the person I'm after!" "Oh," he says,
And yawns, "Gee, but I'm tired. I've been studying.
I have to take my bar exam next week."

"A bar exam!" I make a snappy answer,
"What won't them prohibition-hounds do next?" —
Makin' a joke, you know. He never smiles.
But I start in again, so he can't go.
"Listen. I want to ast a favor of you.
I know you're awful busy, but look here:
I got a ticket that I want to give you.
We open cold, you know — I mean, we open
Here in New York; we don't go to the sticks.
Tomorrow night we open, and this ticket
Is for the show, tomorrow night, ninth row.
It's a real good show, honest. Won't you come?"
He just looks bored, and says, "I can't afford it;
And anyway I don't like music shows."

"Afford it, nothin'," I says, "I'm givin' it to you.
Won't you please take it? I got the biggest surprise
You ever seen, for you. Please, won't you come?"

He says, slow, "Well, all right." So then I stick
The ticket in his hand, and says, "You might

Just come around behind, after the show.
And — I wouldn't mind if you should bring me home."

Imagine me makin' a play like that for any man!
But there, when you're crazy in love, what can you do?
And when he gives you the high hat, all the time —
I was bound I was goin' to wake him up, I tell you.
I'd make him see that I was really good.
If Long, that I bet has saw a million girls,
Had picked me out — well, it's a cinch there must
Be somethin' about me that would interest men.

v

Well, you know how it was.
The show started off a flop.
The whole first ack, just a mess.
Everybody gloomy and sore,
And not a prayer for it lastin' more
Than a week. But me, did I worry? Ha!

There I am in the dressin'-room,
Jumpin' into that lovely costume —
Just as little as we
Can get away with. And say,
I'm beautiful! I am!
I know it from the green way
All the other girls is starin'.
I know it every time I look
In the mirror.

And so, all the time,
I'm just as cool. Scared?

128

What for?
Ain't Jack out there, ninth row center?
I got nothin' to lose,
Everything to win!

Quick, I'm in my place,
Layin' alone in the sand,
Chin in my hand,
Watchin' the back drop, where the waves
Is slidin' and glidin' in the movie moonlight.
Best set of any show in town.
Big trees bendin' down
Over me; both sides black bushes;
Other side a grass hut,
Black grass, everything black but me.
I'm the white shadow — see?

There goes the orchestra.
Now the verse is startin'.
Harold Chester is singin' it,
Swingin' it
Soft and sweet.
I hate him, but he sure can sing.
The verse is through —
Now he's on the chorus —
Now the curtain that shuts me off is partin' . . .

(Oh, shut up, heart!
Can't I catch my breath?
Sure, You're all right,
Janie, old girl!
Jack's out there,
Did you forget?)

Just for a minute, the audience
Is quiet as death.
Then, right at the end of the chorus,
I hear a noise start to curl
Up to the stage, a sort of sigh
Like a wind goin' by.

Harold is off left, behind a bush,
Still singin'. There's a dead hush . . .
And I get on my feet. . . .

Nothin' but a wild drum,
Beatin' like a big pulse,
" Bum-a-lum-a-lum-bum,
Bum-a-lum-a-lum-bum! " . . .
Back of the scenes the male quartet,
And all the time the drum,
And I'm dancin', dancin' . . .

Come back to Ty-peeee,
  Come back to meee!
Come to our island
  Out in the sea-eeee.
Come where the birds are singing all the day,
Come where the moon is shining on the bay;
  Oh, won't you
Come to our hut in Oomoa,
And we'll ne'er go a-
  Way.
We'll have nothing but love from morn till night,
Beneath those South Sea Shadows white.
So please come back to Ty-peeee,

To Ty-peeeeee
And meeee —

Jack! Jack! It's you I'm dancin' for!
Do you see me, Jack? Look at me!
I can dance, and I'm beautiful!
And it's all for you, all for you!

Our island, Jack, yours and mine,
Nobody else, just you and me,
And the big round moon,
And the little waves,
And the soft sand,
And the black leaves,
And the white shadows, white shadows,
White shadows and love,
White shadows, way beyond the end of the world —

Don't be scared — take me in your arms —
Let me feel you holdin' me against you —
Let me run my fingers through that curly hair —
Kiss me!
Jack, oh Jack! You waited so long —

Crash!

The wild hands, clappin',
The house is yellin',
They're standin' on their seats!

Crash! Crash!

The clappin' — the yells!
Curtains swingin' wide, closin' . . .
Nine bows . . . they won't stop . . .
Louder and louder! . . .

I dance it again.
Twice, three times!
They won't keep quiet.
They won't let me go.
It's a riot!
I can't believe it, but it's so!
I've stopped the show!
Jack, Jack! Do you see?
It's me that's doin' it!
It's Janie Lane! It's me! . . .

VI

(Why ain't he at the stage door?)
"Thanks, Thanks!"
(Don't he care at all?)
"Oh, Mr. Zieglitz,
I can't talk business tonight.
There's *other* managers."
(Where can he be?)
"Well, all right, Mr. Zieglitz,
Maybe, tomorrow afternoon."

"Oh, thank you, thank you, everybody . . .
Oh, Mr. Long, it's you I got to thank.
You done it all . . .
Oh, Mr. Long, don't ast me that tonight . . .

132

I'm all upset . . .
I won't forget, honest I won't.
Goodnight! Goodnight!
Please leave me by. . . .
Come on, Mame!
Yeh, get a taxi . . .
Mame, don't say a word . . .
Don't let me cry, Mame . . .
Mame, where can he be? . . ."

          .   .   .   .

" Mame! Open the door,
And go on up ahead."

          .   .   .   .

" Oh, Mame, hold me tight —
Here he comes — see him?
Look — isn't that him?

" Why, Jack, — it's you —
What're you doin' with that book?
Where —
Where was you all the time?
Ain't you got nothin' to say? "

" What!
What? You never went?
You never — oh, you fool!
You dirty, low-life fool!
You and your lousy studyin'!
Get outa my way!
And I was wastin' my time on you! . . ."

White shadows!
Oh, my God. . . .

I

The empty house yawns gloomily
Up at the empty, cloudless sky;
The scorching August sun-rays beat
On a dull wilderness of heat.

The pump is crumbling, red with rust;
The door is silver-white with dust.
No hay-ricks, joggling homeward, pass;
A chipmunk scuttles through the grass.

The burdock and the ragweed keep
Corners where roses used to sleep.
The crazy windows leer and stare
At ragged trees that once were fair.

And still, beneath that empty sky
It stands in changeless dignity.
Few things I know are quite as grave
As any house — or quite as brave.

II

And still it wouldn't rain!
The rows in the garden was just like deep, dry wrinkles
On an old face that's all pinched up with pain.

The poor peas rattled and coughed in the hot west breeze.
The limas had given up tryin' to climb their poles.
There was hisses like chokin' breaths. . . . That was the
    trees.

It was late in the afternoon, and the wife and me
Stood lookin' out at the parchin', pantin' hills,
When she says, "Look!" And I begun to see
Soft, hazy somethin', like a smoke, start driftin'
Out of the ground, and risin' way up high.
It wasn't mist. It was blue. And besides, the sun
Was grinnin' down, and not a cloud in the sky.

The wife turns round, and she gives a sad sorta smile.
" I know what that is," she says,
" It's the kind of thing the Indians used to think,
I guess you'll say. But that there soft blue haze
Is the souls of all the flowers and little plants
That's been killed by the drought.
They're goin' up to see the Evil Spirit,
To try and find out
If maybe it hasn't had enough sacrifices.
They want to show that they were willin' to give
Their lives for the sake of what the drought might spare,
And ast if it won't let just a little live."

I didn't have the heart for such kid notions as that.
I watched the shrivelin' corn, and shook my head,
And went inside the house, to try and forget
That everlastin' heat, stretched on the bed.

And all of a sudden I was awake again,
And the trees was slappin' the roof, and thunder was roarin',

And, like the bottom fell out of the sky,
The good old rain was pourin'!

III

I wouldn't be Zeke!
What do you s'pose he had the nerve to do?
Of course the drought
Burnt up his garden, and his flowers, too.
But still and all
There was the corn, that wasn't hurt so bad.
And then it hailed,
And beat down every single stalk he had.
Zeke stands out there,
Next day, and like to cries, and hollers, " Hell! '
And shakes his fist
Straight up, and then he gives one awful yell:
" If I was tryin'
To be a God," — (lightnin' 'll strike him, sure!)
" I'd be a God,
And not a durned old whiskered amachoor! "

Almost a week, and not a line from you.
And just a year ago, once every day,
Or three times, even, you would write and say
" I love you! Oh, I love you! It's all true!
It's like a song, our love is. Oh, my dear,
There isn't any minute I don't miss you!
If I could only touch you now, or kiss you!
Things are just flat and stale without you here! "

Oh, yeh? Let's see this note six days ago:
" Not much of any news . . . it's awful hot . . .
I don't do very much. . . . Oh, I forgot;
I went last night with Charlie to a show. . . ."

What was that movie line about " Love's dawn " ?
Where's the waste-basket? Please excuse the yawn.

Sixteen

I was just that month sixteen,
  And you couldn't of believed it was really night
The way you could see the apple-blossoms,
  The moon was so bright.

Now it wasn't account no girl or nothin'
  I could ever get words to tell about,
But the smell and the moon got chokin' me,
  And I just stretched out

In the thin little grass, and all a sudden
  I was cryin' like you'd think I wanted to die;
But it was only just that everything was perfect
  That made me cry.

I was one damn-fool kid, ain't it so?
  But I got plenty hard-boiled since that time,
And the moon — only looks like a paper-bag, say,
  Or a thin dime.

I thought maybe I could stay on the job,
But I didn't guess how I was goin' to feel
With you this far away. The times before,
When I was sure I was in love for fair,
It wasn't hard a bit to get away —
Tell you the truth, I useta be sort of glad,
Because I knew all the time it wasn't real.
But here we're four days out, and it gets worse
The further away we get. It's the real thing
This time. It is! Listen, I just can't stand it.
I got to get some job on land, that's all.

This mornin', when I was lookout, on the bow,
I watched us slicin' through the hard green water;
It made me laugh to see the flyin'-fish
Shoot out, like little airyoplanes, for kids.
And lots of jelly-fish, and porpoises
Real solemn — like old preachers goin' swimmin';
And Portygee men-o'-war, sailin' along
So proud that they could sail their little ships.
I almost forgot you for a little time;
Say! It was good to smell the sea again —
I just kep' grinnin' over bein' alive!

But now, tonight, standin' here in the stern,
I watched the wake behind us, all on fire,
Like it was made of billions of fireflies

That drownded, but their lights never went out —
Remember them fireflies that last night there
When we was walkin' down towards the crick? —
So lovely! Little stars down in the water,
And up above more stars. Beautiful things
Around me, beautiful things inside of me,
Because I love you so, and you love me.

I never guessed that love could be like that —
It's sort of holy, like, and clean, and all.
The way you want to start in singin' hymns . . .
While I was watchin', I got thinkin' how
Maybe it might be better, while it's perfect,
And all so beautiful, just to — you know — quit.
I mean — keep it the way it is — our love
Like now; and never have to take the chance
Of gettin' tired, or lettin' it get stale
And cryin' afterwards because it's gone.
(Ain't love like everything? How can it last?)

— If I should just stand on the rail a second,
And lean 'way over, and slip down in the stars —
But strength is beautiful, too; and bein' strong
Means take your chance, and make it come out right.
They's always hope, as long as you can remember
The quiet way we understood, that night.
We can always keep things like that. What are we scared of?

If you was only here! It's so beautiful!
I won't look any longer: it ain't right.
What right has anything got bein' lovely
If you ain't by my side, and see it with me?

That settles it. I got to quit the sea. . . .

Well, don't you see? I had a box of candy,
And I tore it open, and it looked so fine,
And tasted wonderful! And so I et it,
As fast as I could eat. And when it was gone
I was so sick I couldn't hold my head up.
So the next time I got a box, I says,
" I'll save this one, and eat it little by little;
I'll make it last this time, and I won't get sick."
But mice got in, and ants, and it was ruined.

Ain't there no way you can do with a box of candy?
And suppose it ain't candy, but bein' in love I mean:
Oh, has it always got to be too fast,
So that it's gone right-off, and leaves you sick,
Or else it drags along and gets all stale?
Has it got to be always either one or the other?

I

Yesterday the thermometer was near zero.
It may go up tomorrow. All the same,
Three months of winter yet. I just can't stand it!
The slush, the gloomy clouds, the people sneezin',
Two of the girls at the office have the flu,
And all the extra work! Oh, it's too much!

How can you talk about what's " good " and " bad "?
How can you find out which is which? Yeh, how?

What can you do on twenty-seven a week,
Poundin' a Remington, and givin' half
To Ma, and tryin' to buy decent clothes,
And have a good time once in a while and still
Stay " pure "? That's what I do. I'm twenty-one,
And lots of people say that I'm real pretty.
But what have I got to look forward to?
Get married, yeh, to some of these poor fish
That haven't got a cent, and work and slave —
That's a swell future, ain't it? Me, with dreams
Of all the places that I'd like to go,
And never seen one, yet. Oh, what a life!

You see, I had a little secret game
Ever since I was ten. You take these folders

142

That railroads have, and sit down in a chair
And read, and go all over the whole world.

"Plowin' through emerald waters to the Soo" —
Now, that's the Great Lakes cruise. Or take this one:
"Ridin' the singin' rails into the sunset" —
That one's the line of the Sunset Limited,
Bound for the Golden Gate. . . . You get the idea?
Well, that's the only travelin' I have.
And when I've always been so wild to go,
And see new places, and lovely, far-off cities,
It's fun, all right, to read. But just now, lately,
That East wind howlin' and beatin' against the panes,
And snow — snow — snow —

Five days ago I met this Mr. Kirby,
And he's a millionaire, from Montreal.
He owns a chain of wholesale groceries
That spreads all over eastern Canada.
You see, he buys through us. And so he stops
In here to do some buyin' from old Gannet,
Before he goes to Bermuda, for six weeks.

Well, the other day he has to write some letters,
So Gannet calls for me, because I'm fast
Transcribin', and I like to take dictation.
I watched this Mr. Kirby all the time.
He's just the sort of man I like to see,
Reminds me quite a lot of Pa, you know —
Blue eyes, and a sharp nose, and reg'lar features,
But what is most like Pa, and most romantic,
Is on his temples, where the hair is turnin'
Light grey — the way you read of in the stories.

143

And so I take his letters, all the while
Sneakin' a look at him, and gettin' thrills,
All of a sudden I notice what he says
Ain't makin' sense. And I look up real quick,
And he is watchin' me, and smilin' at me —
Not fresh, you see, but sort of shy and sweet.

I get all flustered. He gets flustered, too,
And coughs, and finishes the letters up
Real sharp. But when I start to leave the room
He coughs again, and says, " Miss uh — Miss uh — "
" Miss Forbes," I says, and smiles. He sort of stutters.
" Oh yes, Miss Forbes. I have a lot more letters
To do tomorrow. Don't you think Mr. Gannet
Might let you take them? " I was pleased, of course,
" Why, yes, sir." Then he coughs again, and says,
" It's seldom I can find a girl, you see,
Who doesn't find the way I dictate hard.
It doesn't seem to worry you at all,
And that is why " — He breaks off there, and coughs
Again. So I say, " Thank you, Mr. Kirby,"
And go back to my desk to type the letters.

Maybe you don't believe my heart was skippin'!
Can y'imagine a man with all that money,
And pretty near forty, and all the experience
He must of had, chokin' up over me,
And not knowin' what to say, and gettin' shy?
" Why, gee, he's just a kid, for all his years,"
I says to myself, and felt all warm inside.

I finished up the letters fast as I could.
But still I had to stay long after closin'.

I took the letters in to Fallon's office,
Where Mr. Kirby give me the dictation,
And put 'em on the desk, and started out,
When somethin' hit my eye. I walked right over,
And before I could stop myself, I snitched it out.
It was the prettiest folder I ever seen;
A lovely beach with blue, blue sky, and water
A lighter blue, like Mr. Kirby's eyes;
And on the beach a fella and girl
In bathin' suits . . . And gee, but it was lovely!
But the thing that got me most was the title of it;
Oh, what a title, with the snow outside,
And the wind like a knife — "Forty-eight Hours From
    June."

Goin' home to Brooklyn, I squeezed the folder tight,
Not lookin' at it, because I was savin' it,
The way you save a special piece of candy.
And I didn't mind the way Ma kept on scoldin'
About me bein' late. I let her rave.
Then after supper, locked up in my room,
I took the folder out, and then — what fun!

"Balmy Bermuda" — that was its other name,
That went right under "Forty-eight Hours From June."
Pages on pages about the coral beaches,
And palm trees, and the birds, and grand golf-courses —
I didn't want to play, of course; I wanted
To just walk on the wonderful green grass,
Knowin' that up in New York, folks was freezin'.
And then, the hotels! Most a dozen of them,
And if they're like their pictures, all of 'em

Are bigger than the Pennsylvania station.
" De luxe accommodations, bath, steam heat,
Superior cuisine, golf and tennis privilege,
Twelve dollars per day, and up, American plan."
Oh, ain't that grand? And then a lot of pictures
Of yachts, and steamer chairs out in the sun,
And the big ships that go there, and the names
Of the hotels are all so beautiful:
The " Princess," " Hamilton," " Bermudiana " —
They drive me crazy, sayin' 'em to myself.

I kept on readin' that folder, over and over,
Till I must of gotten hypnotized, or somethin';
All I remember was dreamin' of golden sands,
All warm and shiny, and walkin' through big hotels
With marble steps, and ridin' on bicycles.
And when I woke up, there was the electric light
Still burnin', and it burnt the whole night long.
Say, but Ma's goin' to rave about the bill!

II

I didn't feel so good, goin' down to the office;
The day was grey, and the wind was somethin' fierce.
A fine thing to wake up to — " Balmy Bermuda! "
But thank the Lord, it was a Saturday,
And only a half-day. But the bunch of work
They handed me sure did make up for it.
I didn't get a chance to think about
The weather, or the cold. I just kept workin'.

Then, about half-past ten, old Gannet rung,
And when I went to his office, sure enough

There was that Mr. Kirby, lookin' cheerful
And twice as handsome, and smilin' very friendly.
" I have a few more letters I want to give you,
And Mr. Gannet says that you may take them,
And give your other work to some other girl."

I ran back to my desk, and grabbed my pad,
And my heart was beatin' fast, wasn't that silly?
And I took the folder, too, hid under the pad;
So we had Fallon's office again to ourself.
And Mr. Kirby starts in very business,
And gives me several notes to Canadian firms,
And then he looks at me, and smiles again.
Then, like he had a good joke all his own,
He starts another letter, " My dear Ann."

That letter goes along, friendly and nice,
But not a bit of love, if you know what I mean.
Just about how he hoped that she was well,
And he hoped she was enjoyin' her stay in England,
And how he thought the school the kids was at
Was a real good place for good colonial boys.
She mustn't hurry back on his account,

But he might join her in London, in the summer.
Oh, sure, you guessed it — it was to his wife.
I thought it was funny a man should write to his wife
Dictatin' the letter. . . . And that's the point, you see;
Because, when I got through, and was thinkin' about
Him bein' married, and not likin' his wife,
And told him I'd try to have the letters done
Before he left for lunch, he smiles again.

And says, " On second thoughts, don't bother about
The last one. You may simply tear it up."
A-ha! I knew it all the time! He only
Wrote it to tell me that he had a wife,
And wasn't very crazy about her. Gee!
Aren't men the simplest? But it was sort of cute.

There wasn't any mistake about it now.
I knew he was tryin' to get intimate.
But he was goin' about it nice, wasn't he?
And he was real handsome, with his temples grey,
And yet that real young face. Of course I could
Of stopped the whole thing there. But somethin' made
Me flirt a little, just curious, I guess.
I swear, I'm not that kind. I never flirt,
Honest, I never do. I'm real cold, even,
And if old Gannet was like lots of bosses
That like to get handy every now and then
I would of got the gate long time ago.
Well, never mind. . . . I started towards the door,
Then I turned back, and hauled the folder out,
And says, " Oh, Mr. Kirby, please don't mind,
But I borried this last night, when you was gone."

His face lights up, and he waves his hand, and says,
" Keep it. But why did you want it, anyway? "
I says, " I like to read about those places;
Gee, but I envy you, goin' down there,
With balmy winds, and beautiful soft skies."
He stands and looks at me for a few seconds,
Then, " Look, Miss Forbes, I like you. Very much.
I get so sick of the regular sort of people —

And you're so very different. No, don't smile;
I know that sounds like things you've heard before,
But I'm in earnest. Yes, you're really different.
You have a — well, call it a point of view.
It isn't in what you say — you haven't said much —
It's something in the way you hold yourself,
And a twinkle in your eyes, when they're not dreamy,
And — anyway, I'm feeling terribly bored
With all the usual things I have to do.
Have you an engagement tomorrow afternoon? "

Well, there it was. I s'pose that was the time
For me to stop things short. And for a second
I thought it over, wonderin' what to do.
You see, Al had his reg'lar Sunday date,
And prob'ly would be awful sore at me
For standin' him up. But Al! What does he matter?
Clerk in a cigarette store! And he thinks he's funny —
Just a wise-cracker. . . . That's the only sort
Of boys I ever know, it seems to me.
Thinkin' of Al made me all sick inside,
And before I really meant to, I says, " No,
I haven't got a date."

                    " That's fine," he says,
I'll meet you anywhere you say. If it's clear,
We'll go for a walk. Or I can get Gannet's car,
He has an extra roadster. How would that be? "

" Think you could ever find your way to Brooklyn? "
I asts. He laughs, and says he's sure he can.
So then we fix it up that he's to meet me

149

Flatbush and Fulton at three, because, you see
I didn't want him drivin' up to the house,
Ma's so peculiar, and so awful nosey,
And Al might some way be hangin' around.

So it was settled. But as I went to the door,
He calls out, " Just a minute. You forgot
The folder, didn't you ? " and hands it to me.
And just that sort of seemed to seal the bargain.

III

You wouldn't be very interested in hearin'
About what happened before next afternoon.
Except I bought a hat — that peachy one
At Gimbels', that I'd wanted for a month,
And it sure did knock a chunk from the old bankroll,
But I just couldn't resist it; I wanted to look
As pretty as I could when I met Mr. Kirby.
Can you believe it ? Me, that watches my step,
Gettin' excited over a married man ?
And I *was* excited, too. And very happy.

Erma kep' astin' me questions. Her and me
Was window-shoppin' the rest of the afternoon,
On the Avenue. Oh, and the wonderful clothes
We looked at. . . . And the strings of pearls, and di'-
    monds! . . .
Well, anyway, she was suspicious because
Even though it was colder than Charity,
I didn't complain the way I usually do.
But she didn't guess what I was thinkin' about.

150

I was so happy I kidded Al along,
And made him change the date to takin' me
To the movie that night. And I was nice to him
So he didn't know what to make of me, he said,
And ast me to marry him again — that's twelve
Or maybe thirteen times this year already;
And I wasn't half as mean, sayin' no to him,
As I am generally. And he was pleased,
And thinks he's " makin' progress," so he said.
I don't need to tell you about Ma
Naggin' all Sunday mornin', about why
Couldn't I stay at home all afternoon,
And help her fix a supper for the Somers
And the McQueens, that was comin' over later.
That's Ma all over. Naggin' all the time.
And she wanted to know what was so very important
That I was dressed up, with a bran-new hat —
Where was I goin', and who was I goin' with?
And so-on and so-on. I got nearly crazy.

A quarter to three, and I'd be late, I knew,
If I couldn't shake her off. And so I promised
I wouldn't come back a second later than six,
And that I'd stick around all evenin' and help
Her entertain that flock of terrible owls.
I didn't want to promise. I should say not.
Supposin' Mr. Kirby wanted to take me
To some swell place for supper? But, you see,
It was the only way to shut Ma up.
And so I hurried off, fast as I could,
With Ma still yellin' at me, " Six o'clock!
And don't you dast to be one second late! "

I was so mad, I even took a taxi,
A dollar and a half! Just goin' wild, I guess.
And I got out a block from Flatbush and Fulton,
And paid the man myself. Because, you see,
I didn't want Mr. Kirby to think I was tryin'
Any gold-digger tricks. I ain't that kind.

IV

Well, there he was, standin' next to the subway,
And with a derby on. The only man
I ever saw that could wear one and look fine.
He was just grinnin' all over. " Ah, young lady,"
He says, " I got here fifteen minutes early.
That ought to show how much I think of you! "
And then we go to where the car was parked,
And it was just the cutest Cadillac roadster —
Can y'imagine old Gannet in a roadster?
So Mr. Kirby tucked me in all snug,
And off we started, out to Prospect Park.

I didn't say a thing. He didn't, either.
We just sat there, and let the cold breeze nip us.
Somehow, it wasn't freezin', any more;
It stung, but it was just delicious stingin'.
And overhead there wasn't a single cloud —
One of those spicy days, that look like glass.

Just as we got to the Park, I had an idea.
" Say, Mr. Kirby, drive where I tell you, will you?
I got a little plan. We'll have some fun."
He laughs, and says he will. And so we go

Up to a big brown buildin'. I says, " Stop."
So then, we go inside, he lookin' puzzled,
Until the hot air suddenly smothered us,
And the ripe smells of leaves, and little flowers.

That was a sort of a trick I was playin' on him;
I wanted to see if he'd say somethin' dumb,
The way Al did, the only time I wanted
To go with him into the Flower House.
But Mr. Kirby wasn't that way at all.
He took a great big sniff, and grinned all over:
" Why, that's the quickest trip to South America
I ever heard of. Is this a regular trip —
I mean, is this one of your folder schemes ? "
Now, wasn't that grand, his seein' the point so quick?

We walked together down the paths, between
The great big palms, and the banana-bushes,
Or maybe they're trees — well, anyway, we came
To my favorite place, up at the further end,
Where there's a little seat among the rocks,
Right in the ferns, and nobody was near us.
I guess it was too cold out for lots of people.
There couldn't of been a dozen in the place,
And they was mostly down about the middle,
Watchin' the man feedin' the gold-fishes.
The air, so warm and thick, like you could cut it,
And dreamy-smellin'; and a little stream
Was tricklin' out of the rocks, right near our head,
And it sounded just like a ex-ylophone.
We sat there listenin', maybe fifteen minutes,
And not a word. And I didn't mean to speak

1 5 3

When I finally did. The words came out theirself:
" It's like we was sittin' in a different world,
And like a dream, that both of us is dreamin'.
The winter's gone, the whole world's gone away."

Honest, I didn't know I'd really said that,
Until he answered, in a real soft voice,
" Miss Forbes, I'm glad I found a girl like you.
I don't look like the sort of man who likes
To play, and make-believe, and all that stuff,
Do I ? But that's exactly what I am.
Nobody would believe it. Why, at home
They call me ' Stick-in-the-mud.' Because, you see,
Nobody guesses what I'm really like.
My wife — well, Ann's a woman in a thousand;
She's a fine wife and mother. Runs the house
Perfectly. . . . And she's very conventional.
In all these years she doesn't know me a bit.
I never dare to let myself go, with her.
She thinks — she thinks I'm just a stick-in-the-mud —
A regular, conventional money-maker,
Who never does a foolish, silly thing.
This Flower-house business is so silly, isn't it —
But there isn't anything I'd have rather done. . . .
I can't imagine Ann ever thinking of it."

With that, he gives a sigh. I felt real guilty.
" Oh, Mr. Kirby," I says, " You know you oughtn't
To say such things to me, about your wife."
Only I couldn't sound just like I meant it.
He was such a kid, such a big, handsome kid.

" Oh, what's the use of lying? Ann's all right,
She's a fine woman. . . . But she rather bores me.
And that's the truth. . . . Why, all my life I've tried
To find some person who would play with me,
Who has taste, and is pretty, and has — dreams.
And now, to think I've found just such a person! "

" Oh, Mr. Kirby! You mustn't say things like that!
I'm only just a stenographer, and you're
A millionaire, that's got a wife, and kids."
" I'm not a millionaire," he says, " And you're a dear,
And very, very pretty. . . . And that hat!
Where did you manage to find the very one
That would look best on you? "

                         Well, there you are.
How can you think of what you ought to think of,
When a swell man notices everything,
And shows he thinks you're fine, and really means it?
In a few minutes, I was tellin' him
All sorts of things I never, never thought
I'd ever tell anybody in the world.
All about Pa, and how he'd been a sailor,
In the last days of sailin'-ships. And how
He used to tell me stories all the time
About his voyages to far-off lands,
Before he quit the sea and married Ma.
And how I guessed maybe it was Pa's stories
That started me on travelin' in my mind,
Usin' the folders. . . . And, oh, lots of stuff.
I talked and he talked, and it was so beautiful!

And he told me about his own pretendin'
To travel, same as me; and how he never
Had got the chance to go over to Europe
But once, and that was when he was real young;
But since he'd been a man, he'd had to work
So hard, buildin' his business up; and now
It was built, of course he went all over
In Canada, and the United States,
But he couldn't get to any foreign countries,
And how he was goin' to Bermuda the first time,
Because he could get back home inside of three days,
If anything went wrong. He was excited
About Bermuda. Only he said some friends
That went there quite a lot told him it wasn't
As warm as all the ads kept sayin' it was.
But just the same, it would be marvelous,
And just like June in Canada, anyways.

All this don't mean so much to you, I guess,
And I can't tell it anything like it was.
This is the point: we sat there two whole hours,
And it was just like all our life we'd waited
For somebody to pour it all out to.
He wasn't a millionaire, married, with kids,
And I wasn't just a stenographer, and poor,
He was a man that was lonely, and always had been,
And handsome, and like a kid. And I was a girl
That he liked, and liked him, and we was friends,
And yet not friends, exactly. You aren't excited
And out of breath, and happy half so much
When you're just friends. . . . It was somethin' bigger than
    that.

All of a sudden I saw how dark it was gettin',
And made him look at his watch. So he let go
My hand that he was holdin' — sure, he was,
And I was squeezin' his. Oh, don't you see,
That wasn't anything, the way we felt? —
And looked, and it was twenty-five to six.
And just that minute the man in charge came up,
Growlin'. " All out! " he says, in a mean voice,
" It's five minutes after closin' time, right now."

" Oh, gee," I says, " I've got to run, this minute! "
" Why, don't be silly," Mr. Kirby says,
" We're going to the City right away,
And have the finest dinner we can find."
" I can't. I simply can't! Ma made me promise
I wouldn't be one second later than six."

" Oh, that's all right. Just telephone your mother
You won't be home."

                    " Yeh, that sounds good and easy.
But you don't know my Ma. It would spoil everything!
I'd never hear the end of it. I can't! "
By this time we was almost to the door.
He turns around, and looks back at the place,
And takes my hand and squeezes it again,
And whispers, " Thanks! It was so nice."

And then we get out to the Cadillac,
He helps me in, and starts it up. " All right,
I wouldn't do a thing to start a row.
Where do you live? " I told him. Then he says,

" I'll get you there. It's only twenty blocks,
You say? But let's just stop here in the park
A minute or so. We've got to see that moon."

We were on a curve, and not any traffic near.
He stops, and puts his arm over my shoulder,
And pulls me over, real gently, so I could see.
I had to sort of bend, to get a look,
And leaned against his coat. The cloth was rough,
And it smelt healthy, and like good cigars,
If you know what I mean. It was delicious.

" Isn't it glorious? " Mr. Kirby whispers,
" But it's a dying moon . . . it's going fast,
Just like our day . . . and just like everything
That's beautiful." He gives a little sigh.

I felt so sad. He was such a kid, you see;
I couldn't help it, I just leaned over a little
And put my cheek against that warm, rough coat,
And then he tightened his arm around my shoulder,
And before I realized it, there was his face,
Coming down toward mine, and I was glad.
And then we kissed. . . .

                         Now, I don't mean to say
That no man ever kissed me before. How silly.
But all the rest were just kid-kisses, or jokes.
But this — it was like flames was in my eyes,
And all the orchestras in all the world
Was playin' some wild piece. . . .

V

How long it was like that, I couldn't tell you.
I only know I didn't want it ever
To stop. I didn't care if the world ended.
What woke us up was a voice, right at my elbow.
" Say, what the hell do you think this is? " it said,
" A public neckin'-ground? "

                    Gee, what a crash.
I jumped, and looked to see what was the matter.
But Mr. Kirby, he was furious.
He got right out of the car, and walked real quick
Round to the cop, and ast him what the devil
He meant by gettin' insultin' to a lady.
Then they had words. The cop was awful sassy,
The way cops always are. And Mr. Kirby
Started in calm, but he got madder and madder.
Then what did the cop do but ast for his drivin'-license.
And of course he didn't have one. So the cop
Finishes up, " All right, you come with me.
We'll take a little ride to the station-house."
And nothin' that Mr. Kirby could do or say
Made any difference.

              He came around to me,
As sweet as he could be, and says, " I'm sorry,
Miss Lucy, I certainly do apologize.
There's no way out. I must go with this officer.
And you'll be terribly late. But here — I know.
I'll stop the first taxi that we come to, and
You can dash home. I'll straighten this matter out."

So then we trailed along out of the Park,
The cop chuggin' along, hangin' on to the fender.
You know, it's funny, I didn't feel ashamed
One bit. I was mad for Mr. Kirby's sake,
And sorry our afternoon was endin' that way,
But I was still drunk and dreamy from that kiss,
And sort of desperate to think that he
Was goin' away — just when I'd got to know him!

We stopped a taxi, and he put me in it.
The cop was grinnin', nasty, by the curb.
And Mr. Kirby leaned inside the window,
And says, " Please, please don't be annoyed.
And thank you for the pleasantest afternoon
I ever had. I'm writing you a note.
You see, I have to be in Philly tomorrow,
And Tuesday. But I've something I want to ask.
Good-bye, and thanks. And . . . you're a lovely kid."

VI

All the way home in the taxi I didn't think,
I just laid back in the seat, and closed my eyes.
What had I done? Had I gone and fell in love?
And fallen hard? For a married man, with kids,
And one that was so far out of my class?
Well, if I had, what did it matter, anyway?
I could still smell that warm tobacco-smell
Of his rough coat, and feel his arms around me.

Ma was just terrible. It was half-past six,
And the comp'ny was there already, sittin' around.

She was sweet as honey in front of them, of course,
But in the pantry, dishin' potato salad,
She gave me the biggest bawlin'-out! Oh, Lord!
It must of made her twice as mad, because
I didn't answer back. I just kept smilin',
Thinkin' about the happy afternoon.

So I got through the evenin', bein' nice
To all those hens and fools. And when they left,
I let Ma rave for an hour and a half,
Without a word, about what a terrible daughter
I was, that never thought of anybody
Except myself. Oh, well, what is the use?
When you get nothin' but that, day after day
Five years, you miss your Pa, and understand
Just why he drank so much when he was alive,
And didn't seem to care when the pneumonia
Hit him, but just gave in, and died. Poor Pa!

The spell was still around me, goin' to sleep,
And I kept dreamin' about that Mr. Kirby.
But yesterday mornin', when I first woke up,
It was all changed. I just felt miserable.
Because I couldn't get him out of my mind,
But what could ever come of it? Why, nothin'.
He'd go away — his boat was sailin' Thursday,
He was in Philly now, would come back Wednesday,
And what would happen if I went somewhere
To dance, before he left? For him, I was
A cute girl, maybe, — sure, but that was all.
And so he'd go on down there to Bermuda,
Swept by warm breezes, with the birds and flowers,

And I'd go down to the office every day,
And pound the Remington, and then back home
To rotten Brooklyn . . . and think about his face.

All day at the office I kept thinkin' about it.
And by the time I crawled into the sheets,
I had it all doped out. The thing was finished.
Wednesday, he'd be there. Well, I wouldn't be.
I couldn't stand to see him, ever again.
I'd make out I was sick, and stay away
Until he sailed. . . . And then, after a week,
Or anyway, after a while, I could forget
That afternoon, and how he looked, and how
It felt to have him kiss me. That was that.
A girl like me can't play with fire that way.
And so, I got it all settled and finished,
And went to the office this mornin', calm, and cured.

VII

The first thing when I sat down at the desk,
What do I see but a letter. I read it, quick,
And all day long it's been like I had fever.
I couldn't think, I couldn't hardly eat.
I'm tryin' so hard to figure out what's right,
And make my heart shut up. . . . Here is the letter:
" My dearest Lucy:
                    Yes, that's what you are,
The dearest little girl in all the world.
I can't apologize enough for exposing you
To that fool's insults. Well, but let's forget them.
Hereafter, you can trust me thoroughly;

I'm nothing if not thorough. Here's a plan:
I'm going to take you with me to Bermuda.
I need a private secretary. So
I asked old Gannet if he would loan you to me
While I'm down there. He was delighted, and said so.
I also said my sister's going along.
And so she is. I didn't say that she
Is quite an invalid, and stays in bed
All day as well as night. And we won't see her —
At least you won't. Your salary will be
Any sum you think fair. That lies with you.
There will be correspondence, quite a lot.
And cable-grams, and numerous details,
Enough to keep you busy an hour a day.
But it's the glorious times we're going to have,
In the warm sunshine, bathing in the surf,
Going to dances at the big hotels,
Playing, just playing. Won't it be wonderful?

" I've cabled for a splendid room for you,
Not far from mine. You shall have every comfort.
And let me say, you'll have a charge account
At all the shops down there. I understand
You can get beautiful things, for evening wear
And clothes, too. Anything else you wish
Remember, all you have to do is ask.

" You can't say no, Lucy, you darling kid.
You see how well I've managed it for you.
Old Gannet's O. K. ought to fix it up
At home. I'm sure it will. Didn't you say
Your mother thinks the sun rises and sets

In Gannet? And you know my reputation —
' Old Stick-in-the-mud.' So make your plans at once,
And meet me at the dock, pier 42,
Thursday, at noon. And don't dare to be late.

" In haste, and looking forward to a romp
That will make up for all the years you've longed
To travel, you sweet kid, believe me, ever
Your friend
                                        LLEWELLYN KIRBY."

Isn't it like a beautiful fairy-tale?
I just told Ma, and, because of Old Gannet
Givin' it his O. K., she thinks it's fine,
Even if she does say that she doesn't see
Why she can't go along. . . . Of course, she can't,
And I can see she won't make any trouble.

To get away from all this slush and snow,
And dirty Brooklyn houses, and the office,
Into — where is that folder? — " into lands
Where azure skies hang above emerald hills."
Oh, beautiful!

                    But how would it end up?
" I've cabled for a splendid room for you —
Not far from mine " — Oh, but those warm, sweet nights,
Under the stars — and his hair, over his temples,
All grey, and so romantic — and the way
That kiss still burns. . . . And still, I know, I know
That me or things will never be the same
Again. Six weeks of livin' in heaven, and then —

Listen to the wind, howlin' against the pane! . . .
" Forty-eight Hours From June." . . .

                              What do I care
What happens afterward? I only have
One life. . . . I'm goin' to live! . . . Where is my pen?
Flowers, and birds, and grass. . . .

                    VIII
                    " Dear Mr. Kirby, . . ."

There was the times that I would be with you
When both of us would be funny and gay,
And everything would look all bright and new,
And we would sing, and joke, and laugh, and play.

There was the times that only touchin' hands
Would make us tremble. And it would just seem
Like we was goin' crazy, wantin' each other,
And love would be a wild, sweet, flamin' dream.

But what I remember was most beautiful,
Was sittin' close together, in the gloom,
And not a word. Like when it's quiet, in church,
And you think God is comin' in the room. . . .

Spring never came at all.
   Cold rain every day.
What good did it do to cry?
   What good did it do to pray?
No winds full of flower smells,
   Or nights with a warm round moon —
Not one of the things we loved —
   Snow! — When it almost was June!

We wanted the Spring so much!
   We hoped and waited so long!
Tryin' to fight our troubles,
   And everything goin' wrong;
But even when they was hardest,
   And it seemed like our nerves would crack,
We'd say, " But Spring can save us —
   In Spring it'll all come back! "

But Spring never came at all.
   Nothin' but clouds and cold
And then the blazin' summer.
   And I can't ever find the old
Shine that would be in your eyes;
   And they's only a sort of a pain
Instead of the dreams I had. . . .
   Will it ever be Spring again?

Afternoon Tea

(*A Polyphonic Juvenility*)

You curve, white against the green cushions, on the window-seat. I sit opposite you, uncomfortably neat. April breaks in waves through the wide-open windows. You chirp of this and that, while the maid, very staid, moves noiseless, like a cat, with the tea. On that tree buds are pouting, and I can feel the sap shooting in its tendrils. . . .

And "Don't you think Town Topics is just dreadful?" you say. . . . And it will soon be May. . . .

The sun is in the west, pouring gold upon the curve of your breast, so that a lump is in my throat. A pagan note sings in my ears. A boat faintly gleams on the horizon, bound — who knows? — for Troy or Colchis, full of strong youths with long yellow hair. The smoothness of your ankle stabs me like a knife. Oh, Helen, and Paris, and the long, bitter strife for one devastating passion! . . .

"I really think tight skirts will be the fashion. . . ."

An old, wistful earth-tang pervades the air, mingles with the faint, swooning perfume of your hair, tugs at me, as it were the odor of some forgotten Hesperidean flower. I see poppies rippling, and a myriad exotic blossoms that breathed in an hour when Hellas was young.

And you and I have flung away the shackles of the years. There is no tea, nor whirring wheels of automobiles, nor owl-eyed fears — We are free! We are free!

The petals crush beneath our dancing feet. Io!

A hundred nymphs and satyrs, wheeling, leaping in a mad, glad riot of the Spring. Sing!

Io!

I am drunk with April and your lithe whiteness! Oh, shimmering brightness! Strain lips against lips, body against body! Cling! . . .

"Why, you haven't touched your tea," you chirp to me. "My dear, what a queer look. . . . You know, I've read the sweetest book. . . ."

Stars! —
If they could have a smell like flowers —
White, soft, sparklin',
So beautiful they hurt you —
Not proud and grand,
Just little and friendly —
Crowds and crowds of friends —

Night time by the river,
Stars all up above us,
Stars every side of us,
Like the whole Milky Way
Fell down around us —

Stars —

If they could have a smell like flowers —

Honeysuckle!

Perhaps it were far better not to know
Beauty. Perhaps one should not ever see
The moonlight shedding silver on a tree;
Or apple-bloom. Perhaps one should not go
Where Spring may thrust her little swords of green
Through strongest armor; nor smell birchen leaves
Smould'ring to incense; nor receive the keen
Flicks of a breeze that stirs the new-bound sheaves.

Perhaps one should but guess how two may stand
Merging their spirits by the clasp of hand
In hand, while in their inmost hearts they hear
A far-off swooning music drawing near. . . .

Perhaps he is more fortunate, who goes
Dreaming and wondering, and never knows.

⚡ TO YOUTH ⚡

This I say to you.
Be arrogant! Be true!
True to April lust that sings
Through your veins. These sharp springs
Matter most. . . . Afteryears
Will be time enough for sleep. . . .
Carefulness . . . and tears. . . .

Now, while life is raw and new,
Drink it clear, drink it deep!
Let the moonlight's lunacy
Tear away your cautions. Be
Proud, and mad, and young, and free!
Grasp a comet! Kick at stars
Laughingly! Fight! Dare!
Arms are soft, breasts are white,
Magic's in the April night —

Never fear. Age will catch you,
Slow you down, ere it dispatch you
To your long and solemn quiet. . . .

What will matter then the riot
Of the lilacs in the wind?
What will mean — then — the crush
Of lips at hours when birds hush?

Purple, green and flame will end
In a calm, grey blend.
Only . . . graven in your soul
After all the rest is gone
There will be the ecstasies. . . .
Those alone. . . .

The house is quiet. Everybody's settled
Down to a nap, or talkin' very low
And lazy. It's the restin'-time of day.

And so, of course old Flanders has to run
And stand at the screen-door, starin' and bristlin',
And whirlin' round, and whinin' high, and tremblin',
Tryin' to make me come. He keeps it up
Till one of us says, " It's a woodchuck, sure! "
So then I go, while he jumps up and down,
Barkin' and growlin', clawin' at the screen,
And likes to bust it down before it's open.

Then — whoosh! He's out. Two jumps, — three jumps —
      four jumps —
Slower — and then he stops stock-still, and stares,
And both his ears drop down, and his tail hangs,
And he looks cheaper than a lead half-dollar.

" No? No? " he says, plainer than any words,
" No woodchuck after all? I won't believe it! "
But soon he sneaks off, very hurt and sad.

Well, we're disgusted, too. We settle down
Again, makin' some sour jokes about it.
" Old Flanders, and his woodchucks! " So it's quiet
All of five minutes.

Then we hear a scratchin'
Against the screen, and whines, and frantic barkin'.
It's him again. He scratches and he yips
Till I get up, and swear, and open the door.

So he comes rushin' in, with eyes poppin'
Like he was goin' to see a whole new world
Inside. . . .

            But in a second he can tell
It's just the same old room, the same old folks,
The same old everything he's seen for years.
And so he plops himself down in the corner,
And sighs, and grunts, and lies there, very gloomy.

Then, in a couple of minutes — the same thing!
Bouncin' and quiverin' at the outside door, .
And tearin' out, and always findin' — nothin'.
Then wild to get back in, crazy-excited,
And — nothin' inside either, that's any different. . . .

What do you s'pose he really hopes to find,
Inside, or outside? Why, there hasn't been
A woodchuck on the place for two or three years.
And inside, nothin' changed for longer still.

" Just the same, there was woodchucks once! " He says
To himself, I think. And he remembers how,
Streakin' across the field, fast as a flash,
He nabbed one. . . . And the wonderful crunch of jaws
Makin' it sure! . . . And then the standin' before us,

Bustin' with pride, and lookin' from it to us! . . .
And he remembers when the house was new,
And everything had got to be examined;
And all the fun of passin' things, " O. K."
And chasin' balls was still a brand-new game,
And the dog-biscuits had a strange, fresh taste,
And all the world was worth the sniffin' into. . . .

" Was? " did I say? What am I talkin' about?
His speed is slowed, his whiskers is all grey,
And yet — the wild excitement, every minute!

For him, our rooms are always magic rooms,
Stuffed full of wonders that might start to happen
Any time now! Some game he never heard of,
Or biscuits — not the same old bone and meal,
But some new kind, like somethin' out of heaven.
And, just around the corner, there's a woodchuck,
As big and easy as a cow, he's sure!
And then the glory of gettin' his teeth down in it,
And knowin' he's conquered it, and luggin' it back
For us to see, while his eyes shine and shine! . . .

Oh, Flanders, once I looked for some new game
In every room . . . and magic biscuits. . . . Oh,
And woodchucks, woodchucks just around every corner! . . .

And Who Would Not Envy Me?

When I went loveless,
  Sweet was my song
Sung to efface the tears
  That all night long
Salted my bitten lips.
Oh, aching, empty years!

One came, who gave her love
  Fair in my hands.
Waking or sleeping,
  Peace at my shoulder stands.
Fled are my daytime songs —
Fled with the nights of weeping.

Well, that's the table. It don't seem much to look at.
Just an old, yellow-oak thing, I suppose you'd call it.
We could have had a walnut one, long since,
Or even mahogany. But then, you see —
Thirty-eight years we had it — thirty-eight years!
That's a long time. It sort of does things to it —
Makes it into a treasure, sort of, don't it?

It was a wedding-present from Sam's father,
It and the six old chairs: four with plain bottoms,
And two with leather seats. I recollect
Like it was yesterday the very first supper
We ate at it. A Monday night it was,
We'd just come back from our honeymoon in Canada.
Sam had made the lease for the tiny house
The week before we got married. . . . Five little rooms
On Locust Street, it was.

All the whole month
We were up there, lazying 'round and going fishing,
And getting used to each other, I was worried.
I didn't see how we'd furnish the dining-room.
I had some furniture from Mother's house,
And Sam had some from *his* flat. But, you see,
There wasn't any dining-table at all.

The minute we saw the room, our troubles were through.
There was this yellow oak, all bright and shiny,
And a note from Father Graham, " Welcome Home! "

I scrambled 'round and got some sort of a meal,
It doesn't matter what. And pretty soon
We were sitting in the chairs facing each other,
So close we could touch hands.

Sam didn't pay much attention to the food.
He kept his eyes on me. You know the way
Newly-weds will go on. After a while
He didn't say a thing for most a minute,
Just looked and looked at me. And then he said,
" Mary, I guess you're about the prettiest girl
Anywhere. And I'm glad the table's short
Like this. It lets me see you all the better."

I had to laugh. " Why, silly, didn't you know
It opens in the middle? There's extra leaves
In the china-closet. We can make it big as we want! "

He looked a little sheepish. He glanced around,
And grinned, and pointed at the four other chairs.
" Oh, well," he said, " We'll have a plenty of use
For all those leaves before we're through, I reckon."

I couldn't half eat for laughing. Yes, and blushing.

See those round dents up there next to my place?
Sallie did that. She was the only one
That hammered with her spoon. She always hammered.
She was the first. . . .

Now, right there by the opening —
That's where Sam Jr. tried to carve his name
One time when he was five — or was it six?
Sam caught him just as he was finishing
The " S." It was a warm night for one bright
Young man, I want to tell you. . . .

Well, of course
We'd put in one of the extra leaves a lot
Before Ben came. The children were forever
Having friends over. But the extra leaf
Was permanent, with Ben. . . .

Then we commenced
To add the second leaf. More friends, you see.
Sam kept moving further away from me,
I used to tell him. And he'd always answer
The same thing every time. " My eyesight's fine!
I can see just as well how pretty you are."
He always said it just as if he meant it. . . .

So the children grew, and the table came to its longest.
Sallie married Tom Thorpe when she was twenty,
And they both lived with us the first three years.
The boys were going to the high-school then.
We made a grand big family, I *tell* you!
All the three extra leaves hardly made room.
Sam at one end, and me down at the other.
Ben, and young Sam, and Sallie and her Tom —
And next to her, De Kalb, in his high chair.
De Kalb was my first grandson. . . .

                                        By that time
We had the big house up on Maple Street.
You can imagine the lively times we had —
The noise — the goings-on — the happiness!
The table certainly got its battle-scars.
Look at that brown burnt place. Senator Gaige
Put his cigar there one election-night.
Senator Gaige, no less! . . .

                              Well, then, Sam Jr.
Went off to college, and a short while after,
Sallie and Tom set up housekeeping in
Their own home, on the Heights. And so one leaf
Came out for good. And we didn't have much use
For the second leaf, except for company
Once in a while. And then, of course, vacations.

It was quite a shock the day young Sam left college
Half-through his second year, and went out west
To California. Oh, you mustn't think
He ran away. We told him he could go,
Although it was a real big disappointment
He wouldn't stay and finish his education.
But he was right, I guess. He made a heap
Of money selling real estate out there.
He comes back once a year for two whole weeks,
With Myra, that's his wife, and their two youngsters.

Then the old table swells back to its biggest.
It's mighty quiet when they go back home. . . .
Ben came and stayed at home almost four years
After he graduated. We kept hoping

He'd be content to settle down for good
Right here, he was doing so well in life insurance.
But that was just the trouble. The New York office
Offered him twice his salary.
                                    . . . So he went. . . .
And the last leaf went out of the table with him. . . .

That's been two years now. Sometimes I start thinking
We ought to take a roomer. Not just any
Rag-tag and bob-tail; but some nice young man
Who needs a good home. . . . It's so quiet here. . . .

I talked to Sam about it the other night.
" My land! " I said, " The table's so little again!
You're right on top of me. Why, you can see
Every wrinkle! "

                    Then he laughed real low,
And put his hand across, and squeezed my hand.

" Wrinkles? " he said, " I don't see any wrinkles.
My eyes have gotten old, just like the table.
I guess that's it. But anyway, you look
As beautiful to me as ever. Why,
I guess you're just about the prettiest girl
Anywhere. . . ."
                    Yes. But still. . . .

Ten o'clock every night this week, and here
It's after midnight. . . . Yeh, some " Merry Christmas! "
Customers mean and sore. . . . My back and arms —
And oh, my feet! My feet! I'm sorry, Joe.
I'll help you with the tree in just a minute. . . .

Get my presents and put 'em 'round, with yours, dear.
Ain't it the cutest set of carpenter tools —
That's a real saw, and plane, too! No, they wouldn't
Gimme much discount. But he'll love it, won't he! . . .

All right. Now here's the Santy Claus, and the tinsel.
There. And it looks real pretty, don't it, dear?
Careful about the candles in the morning! . . .

Come here, Joe. Look at that star, right over the roof!
Gee, when the El is gone, ain't it so still, though?
Ain't it the loveliest star! . . . Oh, Joe, do you feel it?
It's sort of like the city was holdin' its breath,
Or . . . prayin'. . . . Know what I mean? Why say, I feel
Real rested! Oh, it's so beautiful, I wish
We could bring him in. . . . But I guess we better wait. . . .

Oh, Joe! When he sees the tree! And the ball. . . . And the
   tools! . . .

Gramma sits in the corner by the hearth,
Efficient-fingered, placid, and very deaf.
She knits and sews,
And does innumerable handy jobs.
She is a shadow in the shadows,
Contentedly remote,
Pleased to be noticed now and then
With shouted pleasant platitudes.
Ask her about the past.
Press her for facts.
What are facts?

Houses are facts, maybe.
And you and I are facts, and so is Gramma —
Perhaps. . . . And life's a fact. . . . Oh, yes,
And love, and work, and wedding-trips. . . .
So is romance. . . .

Canals are facts. I search for detailed facts
About canals.
Gramma has known canals.
She made her wedding-journey up the Erie.
Now for the facts.

" Oh, yes, the wedding was just after noon.
We drove to Utica, three wagons-full.
From Clinton, yes. Your Grandpa was named Clint,

You know." I knew. "The boat was waiting for us.
We got on board at early candle-lighting."

"The boat — how big was it?" I prod her gently.
She turns the matter slowly in her mind.

"Oh — pretty big. I guess it seemed lots bigger
Than what it really was. At least, at first.
It was so strange, you see, so strange and new.
There we were, setting out for the wilderness,
Two youngsters, leaving all our folks behind us,
And hardly any money to our name.
I wasn't scared — oh, don't think that. Why, Clint
Was strong and fine, and there was the job ahead,
And sixty acres homestead. . . . Still and all,
Some nights when he'd be talking to the captain,
I'd lie there, thinking over everything —
The walls would seem an awful ways away.
But I got used to it. And by the time
We got to Buffalo, the boat seemed smaller,
Lots smaller. It was our first home, you see."

A smiling silence,
Which I break patiently.
"How big? As big as canal-boats nowadays?"

"It's been so long since I saw the Erie — well —
I can't exactly figure. One thing's sure,
It was a whole lot bigger than the one
We took again at Cleveland. That was little."
I abandon the question of size.
"What did you use for power? Horses, or mules?
Or did men pull it?"

On this point she was positive, " Not men.
Horses, I think. Or — maybe it was mules.
But it wasn't men. There was only Clint and the captain,
And a funny, dried-up fellow that drove the mules —
Or horses. . . . Anyhow, he was a case.
Chewed tobacco, and never spoke a word,
Not even to the — animals. . . . The captain,
He liked to talk. He was a handsome man.
Not near as handsome as my Clint, but nice.
I can see all the three of them right now,
Dressed up for Sunday, in their flowered waistcoats.
Men don't know how to dress up nowadays.
Clint certainly looked stylish, with his hat —
A big grey beaver — and the heavy watch-chain,
All solid gold, that was. It was the only
Real valuable thing we had. And I,
I'd wear my shoes — silk shoes. My Clint made those.
He was a shoemaker by trade, you see.
A piece left over from my wedding-gown,
That's what he used. There's another in my scrap-book.
You saw it often. We made a pretty couple,
Going to church some place along the way.
That's what the captain was always saying —
' A pretty couple,' yes, that's what he said."

I let her rest after this long description.
I try a feeble joke: " And did you see
Niagara Falls? " But that's no joke to her.
The facts are what she clings to. Yes, the facts.

" Oh, no! We took a little sailing ship
The afternoon we got to Buffalo.

189

We didn't even stay to see the city.
It was a freighter. Not a passenger
But us. Five days it took us going to Cleveland,
Or was it six? I didn't like it much,
I can't remember. I was pretty sick.
It felt so good to get on a canal
Again — the little boat this time. We went
Up to a place called — well, now, I declare —
The name's just gone. It was real near Coshocton.
Only two hours by stage-coach. Then we went
Straight from Coshocton to our piece of land
Across the river, in a place called Roscoe.
Seems like the last part of the trip went quicker —
Quicker than up the Erie, oh, lots quicker."

A fact is peering 'round the corner.
I make a frantic grasp. " How fast? I mean
What speed did those canal-boats make per hour?"

Slowly she speaks, then gathers speed herself.
" Well — you can guess how fast a pair of horses
Could pull a good-sized boat. Or mules. I'd sit
Out on the back with Clint, up on the cabin.
The roof was flat. We didn't go so fast
We couldn't see the trees down in the water.
The willows hung so low you couldn't tell
Where leaves begun and water started in.
My, it was green. The middle west is lovely,
The loveliest place in all the world, in June,
Or anyway, we thought so then. The captain
Of the Ohio boat was a young boy,
Not quite as old as Clint. He was full of fun.

We'd all sit out there nights, he'd play the guitar.
He played it well. And all of us would sing.
Clint had the prettiest baritone! He'd roll
The verses out, and we'd join in the chorus.
The time went quick."

Once more I stab at specifications.
"How were the accommodations? Furniture good?
Beds comfortable?"

"I don't suppose you'd call them wonderful,
But they were good enough."

"Food? It tasted fine." That long, slow smile
Once more. "We didn't notice very much.
We were so happy, being let alone
On our honeymoon, and going off on adventure."

I grin. "I should say so. Now, tell me, Gramma,
How long did it take from Utica to Coshocton?"

She doesn't answer. I wonder if she heard.
In a mild yell I say the question over.

"How long? Why, just a month. Yes, just a month."

"A month!" Why, here's one concrete fact at last.

"A month to a day." She takes her glasses off,
And peers past me into the dark behind me.
Then, with conviction and simplicity
She adds her other fact, her fact of facts:
"Yes. And — it was moonlight all the way!"

Soliloquy

1

(Mother to Girl-infant)

There you lay, so little and young and soft . . .
My baby girl . . . and my big girl some day . . .
How am I goin' to start you the right way
So's you'll get somethin' decent out of life?
Boys can take care of their self; but a girl, now . . .
You got to get the best that's goin', darlin'!
It ain't any cinch, the thing's you're up against . . .

Most folks would say I ought to bring you up
Good, and pure, and innocent. . . . Oh, yes,
" Be good and you'll be happy " — is *that* so?
I'm happy, I guess. Oh, I been good, all right,
And all them other things. And your Pa, yeh,
He's a " good " man — he does the best he can.
I got a roof over my head, and clo'es
Enough . . . none of the dainty things I dream of,
And nothin' fancy about this little flat,
And only movies to go to . . . and a plenty
Of dirty dishes, and always breakin' my back
Tryin' to keep things tidy . . . I don't kick;
It's got to be put up with. And poor Frank,
It ain't his fault. He *is* a good man, too.
Yeh, he is good, and I am good, . . . and so . . .

They's lots of luck about this marryin'.
Take Mary. She's another, lots like me.

192

Always behaved herself, and done her duty;
Nobody ever said a word against her.
Well, and she just kept goin' on, like a mouse,
Quiet and nice, workin' for Mr. Humphreys,
Bein' his private secretary, always
Learnin' more things about his business,
And helpin' him so well, until one day
She got another offer, twice the pay;
And when she told him, all of a sudden he says,
"Mary, I got so used to havin' you
Help me, and seein' you, and talkin' to you,
I couldn't stand it if you went away —"
So now she's Mrs. Humphreys, and she has
A real nice house, and everything she needs,
Even a Buick Coach . . . and a fine husband . . .
Oh, it ain't anything so very grand,
But still and all, bein' good paid . . . for her . . .

Of course, I guess the one that made the biggest
Success of any of the girls I knew
Was Rose. Nobody ever called her good!
My, when I think of how we used to talk
About her pettin' and drinkin' and runnin' around
While we was still just kids! . . . Oh, she was wild,
You bet! And everybody knew the way
She got swell dresses, and the things she did,
And all the men she had . . . but there was somethin'
About her you couldn't help but keep on likin'.
And as for men! — "Say, I can handle 'em!"
That's what she used to tell us. And she could.
She had 'em wrapped around her little finger.
Sure, she was "bad." But still, she wasn't cheap.

She had her own idears, and she stuck to 'em.
And didn't she meet Earl Coles in a cabaret,
And didn't he go completely off his nut,
And didn't she keep him jumpin' through the hoop,
And would he rest until she married him?
Well, now look at her. Money by the ton,
And swell friends — yes, and nice ones, plenty of 'em.
She's happy. Oh, she is! I can tell!
And she behaves — you bet your life she does.

And that Earl Coles is the proudest man alive.
Can't keep his eyes away from her one second.
She loves him, too . . . well, it's a great success,
That marriage . . . Yep . . . she knew her game, and
    played it.

Shall I bring you up to know all about men,
And all about yourself? Ought I to raise you
So you can look at life without a wink,
And punch it in the jaw, and knock it cold?
Shall I make you a Rose? . . .

                And still, there's Mary.
She was a good girl. . . .

                Yes, but so am I. . . .
Oh, what's the answer?

They are always coming back these moon-washed nights —
  The little lost loves —
Through the chinks of the windows, on the soft May
    breeze, . . .
  Something moves

Frail and very delicate, familiar and young,
  Within a corner;
And there's another winsome wraith, silent and abashed
  Like an unbidden mourner.

Only shy bits of them gleam from the shadows
  And tighten my throat;
A brown eye — a honeyed curl — a cheek's curve, pure
  As a thrush-note.

Why must you spy upon me, little lost loves
  Of my youth?
Have you not heard I have found her — my miracle
  Of beauty and truth?

They answer me nothing; they huddle and shimmer
  In the moon's glow,
Wistful and relentless; timidly mocking . . .
  And will not go. . . .

Content and safe, I loll beside the fire,
   And listen to its calm, assuring roar.
It is the end. It is our passion's pyre.
   Against you I have barred the ultimate door.

I have forgotten you. In her alone
   I find the answer to the final question.
This is my life: a household of my own,
   A child, a dog, an excellent digestion.

It is some lie that under a windswept tree,
   Touching your lips, I touched my vanished youth,
And found again a young, new ecstasy.
   It is a lie, I say. This — this is Truth!

Now — I shall rest. For youth and you are gone.
Tomorrow I shall put my flannels on.

When I was young, I always swore
   That stickin' home would never do for me.
I was goin' to be a sailor, or maybe a marine,
   And see everything there was to see.

I useta lay out in the orchard lot,
   And dream about Frisco and the West;
Or China — or Japan — those was better still;
   Or the Amazon — that was the best.

Well, now I drive a truck for the A. & P.
   And the furthest away I ever went
Was out to Chicago, three years ago
   Haulin' freight — but we slept in a tent.

Now I got a little place out at Richmond Hill,
   A little piece of ground with a shack.
Every Sunday I go there with the wife and the kid,
   And we got a sort of garden at the back.

Did you ever watch things that you planted grow?
   Did you ever look sharp all around,
And find somethin' comin' where nothin' was before,
   And see it crawlin' up through the ground?

Say! the funny kind of feelin' that you get all over!
  Like a whole lot of things was new;
And it ain't the plant only that's swellin' and climbin'
  And fightin' for its life — it's you!

Why — all of a sudden there's a singin' in your ears
  That sounds like the roarin' of the sea.
And you're happy — for a minute — and you almost forget
  The kind of man you wanted to be.

So Lucy wants to marry this Marine —
" Wants to "? She's ravin', crazy wild about him;
Her face like it was new-made, twice as pretty;
And every time she says his name out loud
She makes " George " sound as if it was a song.
It's the real thing this time. And who should know it
As well as me? — and now I got to try
To tell her what I think she ought to do.
What can I say? How can I make her see?

He sure is one fine figure of a man,
So big and straight! And curly hair, and eyes
That's laughin' most of the time: and that soft voice
That's just like strokin' you when he is talkin'.
Real gentle, he is. And yet, you know right off
He can turn in a wink to somethin' hard,
And quick, and terrible, that would be awful
To fight against. Somethin' that wouldn't ever
Give in, no matter what he had to go through.

Such a grand record he made in the war!
Wounded, and decorated, and things like that.
And reënlisted right away, and stayed.
And everybody that knows him says that he's
The best top-sergeant in the whole Marines.

But now, with his enlistment runnin' out,
He swears he's through the wanderin' life forever.
" Yes, ma'am," he says to me, " I sure love Lucy.
And what I want is for us to get married,
And have a little home right near your place.
And kids. Back there in nineteen-ten, after
My hitch in the calvary, I worked two years
In the best auto-repair shop in Los Angeles.
I got to be a cracker-jack, even if I
Say it as shouldn't. Now I got a roll
Saved up, and there's this friend of mine, Jack Boals
That's crazy to have me buy in on his shop.
It's a grand business. Just the thing, you see?
I had enough of kickin' 'round the world.
You needn't to worry, Ma'am. I'm settlin' down! "

Talkin' that way and thinkin' of Lucy, he grins
So pleasant-like and tender, I know he means it,
Every word of it — now. And I almost believe
He's always goin' to feel that way . . . almost . . .

What can I tell her? Would it do any good
To say what's in my soul, day in, day out?
How can I put it so she'll really get it?
Like this?: " He's a real man, your George. The kind
That men respects, and women can't help lovin'.
Only — " And how can I say what that " only " means?

How many times I told her about her Pa!
Just such a laughin' happy-go-lucky way
He had; just so he come along one day;
One of the last that sailed the old wind-jammers;

Thirty, he was, with eighteen years of sailin'
In every sea on earth. And he was " through
With rovin' " — so he said. And so he took
My heart for keeps. Oh, yes, he " settled down."
He was a right good carpenter, and learnt
To be an expert quick. And three whole years
It was just like a dream, in our little flat.
And Lucy come. And Jim was always laughin'
So happy, and his eyes laughed too. Oh, yes —

How can I make her look ahead, and see
The way her George's laugh'll sort of fade
Till it ain't real no more? And then, one day,
She'll think he's lookin' straight into her eyes
Like always, and then all a sudden she'll feel
It isn't her he's seein', but some place
Thousands of miles away — And she'll be scared,
And ast him what's the matter. Then he'll grin,
And shake his head, and say " It's nothin'."

So she won't worry again for a few days.
And then she'll notice two or three times a week
While he is talkin', names like " Singapore "
Or " China," or " Haiti " will pop up where it don't
Make any sense. And that same look will come —

So then she'll work and fight to keep him happy.
And doll herself up fine, and take such pains!
It won't be any use. There'll be a silence
Growin' up like a wall, growin' and growin'
Until the minute comes when he can't stand it
A second more. And then it all comes out —

" I hear the surf a-roarin' on a beach
Five thousand miles from here " — those was Jim's words
That cut into my mind like with a knife.
" The wind is singin' songs to me," he says,
" I got to smell the salt again. Oh, hell,
Sure, I'm a fool. This is so sweet and nice
Here in our flat, with you and the kid. But God!
I just can't help it. Oh, I've tried to fight
Against it, but the old life's just too strong! "
What good did it do, the more I begged and begged?

" It's just a little special trip," he says,
" Down in a schooner to South America,
Me bein' skipper for this queer old duck
That's doin' explorin' around some unknown islands.
It's good pay, see? And I got quite some dough
Saved up. It's yours. And don't you worry a bit,
I'll be back soon. But I just got to go —
Just for the change. This life is killin' me,
So slow, and regular, always the same — "

And so he went; and he come back all right,
After six months, lookin' so gay and fine,
The way he used to. And he " settled down "
Again. And this time lasted 'most a year,
Until he got another skipper's job
In coastwise shippin'. But that was too tame
Of course. So then it wasn't but a year
Before he had to go with some crazy fools
That knew the place they was a buried treasure
Off somewheres in the Caribbean sea —

Nobody ever heard of any of 'em
Ever again. And I went back to Pa's,
And boarded with what was saved up in the bank,
And what I managed to scrape up with dress-makin'
Till Lucy got old enough to help, with a job
Typewritin' —

        Oh, don't think it's him I blame!
I couldn't hold him, that's all. No woman ain't
Strong enough to hold that kind of a man.
It only lasts so long. There's somethin' owns 'em,
Those men. It lends 'em to us for a while,
And then — it calls 'em, and they have to go.
Huntin' for treasures — or South Sea islands, or
Alaska — what's the use of namin' places?
Somewheres — where things is happenin', that's it!
They wasn't made to sit and fret at home,
They got to go and do!

        And now, it's Lucy.
" Like mother and like daughter " — that's the way
I guess you'd say it. And it's in the blood
To love that kind. . . . And yet, I got to save her. . . .

Save her? Save her from what? I got no right!
Even if she has to pay with years of cryin',
And nights of layin' wonderin' and prayin',
It's worth it! Oh, it's worth it! To have him love her —
One of the strongest, one of the bravest ones!
None of your pale-faced, creepin' stick-in-the-muds,
But a real man!

             No, I ain't got the right
To say a word. It's her own life. She has
To take her chance. Why, since the world begun,
There's always us, that have to stay behind,
And watch, and cry, and hope — God help us all!

Bowl-and-Pitcher Holiday

(For Dorothy Gish)

No more troupin' with kids for me, that's final.
God knows the life is tough enough anyways. . . .

You see, I'm out with a turkey — " Her First False Step."
This little Dorothy, she's six years old,
And talk about your troupers! There she is,
Sleepin' on day-coach seats, or in hotels
Cockroaches wouldn't live in. And for dinner
Many's the time only one dry ham-sandwich
And maybe a couple of apples . . . and the theaters! . . .
Honest, the lousiest route of one-night stands
Anywheres in the sticks. . . . And Christmas week
Twelve shows. . . . But all the while never a yip
Outa the kid. Brother, that's troupin', that is!

Now, in the last act, it's supposed to be
Christmas, and the kid enters — you remember?
Of course, we never carried a Christmas tree,
But she was supposed to act like it was there.
Well, then, we get to Fond du Lac, Wisconsin,
And, bein' it's really Christmas, the rest of the troupe
They get a bright idea. They're goin' to give
The kid a celebration, to make her happy.
So then, Dorothy's goin' along, as usual,
Doin' her stuff real good. And the third act,
She starts to gallop on for her big scene —

And there's a real tree standin' on the stage,
Lit up with candles, and hung with all the fixin's!

She takes three steps — and her eyes starts to pop.
She stops dead in her tracks, tries to go on
Sayin' her words — and gives a couple of gulps,
And busts out cryin'. And she cries, and cries,
Watchin' the tree. And the audience all laughin',
And me dried up, with lumps stuck in my throat. . . .

Finely, they have to ring the curtain down.
I tell you it ain't fair to have a little
Yellow-haired kid puttin' things in your head, —
Things you gave up many's the year ago.
You got to be hard-boiled to stand the gaff!

Next time, by God, they got to use a midget!

"The Mail's Got to Come Through!"

Around our village, they call him "Goofy Bill."
We're rather harsh of judgment here in Ludlow,
At least, the "woodchucks" are. I'm not a "woodchuck."
I have this farm some two miles from the village,
In the Connecticut hills. And here I stay
All summer, and some years most of the winter,
Making small trips to New York. Thus I'm neither
A "woodchuck" nor a "city guy," but something
Looked at askance by both, and hence removed,
I think, from any native prejudices.

To those hard-bitten, nickel-nursing farmers,
Bill was just "Goofy." For they have no patience
With weaklings. And a lesion in the heart
To them was only a poor excuse for shirking
The plowing, and hay-pitching, and the ordeal
Of scratching out a living from the rocks.
They jeered at him for taking easy jobs,
And said the doctors were a pack of liars,
And even when poor Bill rushed to the draft-board,
Imploring them to take him anyhow,
They said it was a feeble piece of acting.
The girl he had been courting timidly,
Laughed at him at a social, and the next week

Married a corporal in the regular army,
(Somewhat in haste) and went away to Brooklyn.

He talked to me about the girl at times,
Mournfully. He had forgiven her, he said,
And guessed she had been fooled by people's talk.
After his long harangue about her virtues —
A slut whom I had seen two or three times,
And chased, in fact, from off my orchard-lot
Where she was " loitering " with some nameless lout
One evening in the spring — I was inclined
To sympathize with all the local verdict.
Yes, he was " goofy " over several subjects.

His chief obsession was for uniforms.
Within his cloudy mind, he saw himself
Always outfitted in some dashing suit
Furnished by Uncle Sam. And he had tried
In vain the army, navy, the marines —
Every branch which wore a cap and buttons.
Be sure the village wags made much of it.
" Goofy Bill is tryin' to enlist again " —
Such was the weekly joke. . . .

                      Meanwhile he mooned,
And puttered, clerking at the general store,
Drawing starvation wages, teased and bullied.

I seemed somehow to have caught his confidence.
When I would drop in for some trivial purchase,
He fell into the habit of low whispers,
Drawing me to a corner, mumbling quickly
Some sentences relating to " the service."

"Couldn't you fix it? You got influence.
I'm willin' to take a chance about the heart." —
So he would speak, and scuttle to one side
When old man Meadows fixed his glare upon him.

Applejack gave me my opportunity
To give poor Bill his chance. Our usual postman
Habitually managed to be two hours late
Even in sunny weather. And he took
His route as an unpleasant adjunct to
His pleasures, which were mostly bibulous.
I stood his curses and his daily lateness,
But open warfare was the order when
A twelve-pound package was delivered through
My pantry window — which happened to be closed —
With the result that Rural Free Delivery
Number nineteen required a new incumbent.

I pondered several days. Then used my " influence " —
The little I could wield — and in the end
The job was " Goofy Bill's." . . .

                                    And then, ah then
What spasms of laughter shook the Ludlow folk!
To Bill I loaned a hundred dollars, taking
His note for twelve months. Thus with sixty of it
He was enabled to buy old Meadows' Ford —
Of pre-war vintage, sick with all the ills
That Fords are heir to. And with the rest
He had a special uniform concocted:
Grey shoddy, studded with buttons large as hen's-eggs,
Brilliantly brass; surmounted by a cap

Of grey, bearing a label cut in steel,
" U. S. A. Mail." . . .

No knight of old, riding a prancing charger,
Could have gone forth upon the path of Honor
With stauncher pride, with more chivalric ardor
Than Bill displayed, guiding his frantic Lizzie
Upon his mail-deliveries. No more lateness!
Promptly at nine each day the clarion call,
Like some Gargantuan duck, smote on my ears,
And here came Bill, grinding around the corner,
And leaping out, the letters in one hand,
The other touching the cap in a smart salute.

" How do you like the service? " he would say.
Breathless with knowledge of efficiency,
Beaming with joy at any commendation.
And he would point toward the gasping Ford,
And call attention to its polished lamps,
Its shining coat of paint, its gleaming hubs,
Telling me of the hours he had spent
Working upon its surface and its entrails.
" The good of the service! " he would say, " I tell you
I never spare no pains! I got a motto:
' Nothin' else matters; the Mail's got to come through '! " . . .

The autumn passed, and " Goofy Bill " went on,
Grimly oblivious to the hoarse guffaws
Greeting his name about the countryside,
Filling his job even to overflowing.
And then the snow set in, gladdening eyes,
Infuriating souls. Roads became dire,

Scarcely accessible. And Bill's old car
Groaned like a wounded thing. But Bill himself,
His face aglow with zeal, fought through the storms,
And kept his tardiness to a minimum.

"Look here," I'd say, "Why can't you take it easier?
Why don't you wait, these days when it's so bad,
Until the plow can clear the roads? It doesn't
Matter if you're a little late, I'm sure.
You'll harm yourself, taking it all so hard."

He'd stare at me in hurt surprise, and gulp,
And say, "Oh, Gosh! I thought you understood!
It's Uncle Sam! The mail's got to come through!"

It was no use to argue. He was "sot." . . .
I don't believe I've ever seen a blizzard
Worse than the one which started on the night
After the January thaw last year.
All through the hours of blackness, the wind hurled
Great sheets of white upon our barren hills,
Until the whole world seemed one swirling waste,
One frozen madness in the morning's half-light.

I tried to dig a pathway to the barn,
But by the time I'd shoveled twenty yards
My tracks were covered, and the drifts were heaping
Higher than ever, while the tempest shot
Thousands of little arrows into my face.
I gave it up. I sat before my fire,
Relieved and comatose, marooned and free.

"There'll be no mail today," I said to Peggy,
"That crazy boy won't venture out in this.

211

It's a good thing. I thought he looked a little
Worn out from changing two tires yesterday.
That Ford of his is all right for good weather,
But this — I think he needs a bit of rest."

And I was right. For lunch-time came and passed,
And never a sign of Bill. I sat and read.

Along about three o'clock, the telephone
Summoned me. It was the postmaster at Ludlow.
Had I seen Goofy Bill? Why, no, I hadn't.
Why? Well, the damned young fool had started
Out on his route that morning, same as ever,
In spite of all the warnings they could give,
And Mr. Kimball said he had been there
Just before noon, having a hell of a time
Because the car was boiling, and the road
Had drifts across it more than five feet deep —

That was enough for me. Cursing, but anxious,
I called to Frank, my hired hand, to come.
We threw into the Buick several blankets,
Two shovels, and a flask of my best brandy,
And plunged into the blizzard. . . .

It took us half an hour to make Kimball's.
Slithering, shoveling, shoving, scraping the ice
Every two minutes from the coated windshield.
Kimball was loud in his denunciation
Of jackasses who couldn't stay at home
And let the mail go hang. Nevertheless
He joined us in the search. So out we lurched
Upon the back-road leading through the valley.

That trip defies description. . . .

                                Twenty minutes
Down that incredible road, we found the Ford
Down in the ditch, lying upon its side,
Its wheels beckoning in a ridiculous
Appeal. No mail-bag in it. Not a sign
Of Bill. Only the snow lashing and screaming. . . .

We found him in the valley, half a mile
Short of my house, stumbling in a circle
Mechanically. There was a mask of ice
Crusting his face. His eyebrows were pure white.
And from the visor of his silly cap
Hung tiny icicles. . . . He couldn't speak. . . .
He fought me, though, when I made my attempt
To pry the mail-bag from his frozen hand. . . .

He will recover — at least, partly recover.
Six months in bed will mend his tired heart
Enough for him to clerk in Meadows' store,
Taking it easy. He had to lose three fingers
From his right hand. His eyebrows will grow back. . . .

I didn't tell you of the words he whispered
As soon as he could whisper anything.
Of course, you've guessed them. Yes, it was the sentence:
" The mail had to come through! " . . .

                                The mail-bag's contents
Consisted of two post-cards, seven bills
And a Sears Roebuck catalogue. . . .

Italy —
Not the pictorial unreality
Of Vesuvius, blowing his smoke
Into the sky's blue eyes;
Nor the scampering ants
Of Naples;
Nor the virility
Of Rome;
Nor the melodrama
Of Venice;
Nor the blue-gray calm
Of Siena —
Not any town.
The heart —
The nose!

Wait.
The heart, first.

The operatic moon gleamed down
At midnight on the Arno.
Upon a low stone pier
A man munched bread,
Dangling his feet.
No one was near.
He talked to himself aloud

With singing.
His face uplifted to the tinselled night,
He sang full-throated —
Rollicking songs,
Sad songs.
Not for me.
For the moon, perhaps.
For his soul.

I left him.
I slept.
Tumult awakened me.
I ran to the window.
Shutters were closed.
In the white morning sunlight
It marched and countermarched —
A band,
Resplendent in scarlet and gold,
Strutting and clicking
Behind the prancing drum-major.
What were they playing?
Who knows? Who cares?
Earth-shaking, ear-shattering
Happy din,
Rattling the windows
Like an epileptic's teeth.

Children, uttering music
Because music was in them,
Bursting from them.
I laughed,
I wondered.

I laughed,
And tears were in my eyes.

The heart — then the nose.

Remembering,
I started through the mountains.

Suddenly
Wave upon wave of fragrance bathed me.
Simple, frank, gentle,
Naïve as the notes of birds,
As the soft speeches of a child.
Soothing, dreamy, delicate.

With that pungent perfume
Came not understanding,
But feeling.
I did not comprehend —
I knew.
The little man, the lonely band —
The yellow flower.
Italy was unfolding its heart to mine.
Heart of a wildflower.
Ginestre.

To Margaret

How shall I put in words the glory of you?
   How capture hints of your perfection's whole?
   "Your body's loveliness . . . your radiant soul —"
I, so incredibly privileged to love you,

Falter and hesitate. How could there be
   Sentences adequate to catch the grace
   Of spirit shining in your candid face —
Your Being's music, sounding ceaselessly?

"You are all Beauty; you the essential dream
   Poets have clutched for, since the world was new!" —
   See how the petty phrases chirp and coo,
See what a shallow mockery they seem! . . .

Go unsung, then, my love! . . . Give me your hand. . . .
Look in my eyes. . . . Now do you understand? . . .

To My Son

"To follow the dream — and again to follow the dream
— and so — *ewig* — *usque ad finem!*"
—CONRAD'S "LORD JIM."

Must you frown so?
Must you scowl so bitterly?
Oh, I know
It's very strange, after the warm, dark silence —
This cold, confused inanity.
But don't frown.
Nothing lasts forever, be assured.
Only a few years, after all, to be endured;
Then you may go back down
Into the tranquil nothingness.
You have my word.

What can you have heard
While you were where you were?
Did some subtle rumor seep
Into your deep
Calm of nonentity?
Can it be
They have warned you what you may expect?
Did they say how you must grope
With only a hint of what you are groping for?
And fight, and ache, and hope
And only guess what you are hoping for?
Did they say how you will see

Beauty scorned and trampled, and the ugly
Triumph of efficient swine, guzzling smugly?

Oh, it's all true enough.
You will observe
Senseless tragedy, incomprehensible pain.
And you will find you cannot do enough,
Try as you may,
To keep your white integrity
From the world's stain.
And there will be many a tortured night
When you will stare and stare,
And tear
At your own flesh, and toss, and bite
The pillow in your agony,
Because you cannot make your dream come right.
(Do not delude yourself, dear boy;
One does not ever make the dream come right)

But the dream — follow it!
Never abandon it, though the pursuing take you
Into the mire, into the desert places
Where no help is; into the filth and squalor
Clotted with brutish, empty faces;
Into destruction, death.
Not for a moment will you see it clear,
Your dream.
You must not hope to. It is the chase that matters.
Though your flesh become ribbons,
And your spirit, tatters.
Drive! Drive!

219

Follow the dim gleam
Follow!

There will be those who will seek to divert
Your eyes from your dream.
Many will plot and scheme
How they may blind you,
How they may bind you.
And there will be a few
Loving you,
Who will endeavor to guard you from all hurt.

Listen to none!
Yourself, you must fight through!
Defiance to the foe, gentleness to the friend,
But in the end
The way of the dream is the lonely way.
They are they.
You are you.
And what can I promise for a reward?
Is there, then, nothing but the hard
March toward
A will-o'-the-wisp,
With oblivion beyond?

Oh, yes! Along the road that you must go
You will find bits of dream-trail here and there.
Sunsets, and purple dawns, and the slow
Drift of the moon . . . melodies, and
The soft richnesses of women's hair. . . .
And lips that cling and tremble . . . or a hand
Clasping yours firmly, stanchly, joyously . . .

And there are fragrant souls that hide away,
But may be glimpsed by one who seeks . . .
Other dream-hunters, too . . .
And the compelling blue
Of the sea . . . and something that speaks
Out of the earth, in April . . . and the glow
Of ripened fruits, in autumn . . . and the sparkle
Of starlight on the snow . . . and the crisp patterns
That words can make . . . and the sweet curves
Of thighs and breasts . . . and the inscrutable fog . . .
The gay, devoted banter of a dog . . .
The bursting green of the grass, after
The pelt of rain . . . and the brooks' laughter . . .

But — enough.
Search out your own dream-stuff.
It will guide your stumbling soul
Toward the mist-enshrouded goal.

Come, now.
Set out upon your futile quest.
Chase your dream, the while you know
You will never grasp it.
Up, then! Go!
Earn your timeless rest . . .

Must you frown so? . . .

✳ TURNING POINT ✳

" *It's no business of yours whether my heart cries or not;
but I have a mind to tell you, for all that.*"

CANDIDA

Sonnet

Why all this cry for Immortality?
Neither in Fame, nor in the fact, do I
Hope that my name or spirit will not die.
Oh, I shall not go gladly. It will be
With rage that I shall face the Ultimate;
There will be songs unsung. There will be Mays
Not smelled; there will be flaming autumn days
Not seen; and suddenly will cease the spate
Of words. . . . But I give thanks that in the grass,
Among the waves, within the crowded town,
I felt a lyric Something hover down,
And with my senses clear, I watched it pass.
   And if, after long years, one among men
   Should say, " Why, he touched Beauty once! " —
   Well . . . then . . .

"No, you don't get no raise, and you don't get
Moseley's old job in the front of the store, either!
Tell you the honest truth, Saunders, you ain't
Much good no more. You don't earn what you get.
You ain't so active, and you growl too much.
You're lucky I got the patience not to take you
And throw you outa here right on your can."

Saunders' cheeks shook. "Seventeen years!" he said,
"Seventeen years I put in, in this store —"

"Yeh?", Manning talked down into his desk,
"Well, now, them seventeen years is all that saves you.
You can stay on here — same job, and same dough.
But one more yip outa you, and you go
Right out on your can. Get me? Now, scram!"

Saunders groped his way to his hat and coat,
Fighting back impotent tears. Fleming, waist-deep
In Better'nwool Sox and special-sale ties,
Glanced at him kindly. "Go ahead home," he said,
"You look all in. I'll finish with the stuff."

"Thanks," mumbled Saunders. He stumbled through the
      door
And reached the decrepit Ford, beside the curb.

Seventeen years behind those counters back there —
No raise for three — abuse from customers
Ever and always — sarcasms from the boss —
The nauseating, stark monotony —
And what would Minnie say? How could he face her?
"You get that raise — hear me? Now, don't you dast
To let him beat you down, or you and me — "
Those were her parting words that very morning.
And now — not only beaten down, but shown
That keeping him at all was charity.
All true enough, too. Where could he ever find
Another job? It would mean weeks of seeking . . .
Life stretched before him, a terrifying retreat
Toward . . . What? . . .

He wrung the handle of the little car,
With hands that ached and trembled. The old Ford
Quaked into life, at once. He almost smiled.
"Good old Lena," he muttered, "Good old Lena!
Anyhow, I can always count on you!"
His breath stopped, as he found a slip of paper
Upon the steering-wheel. A ticket! God!
The cop had given warning just last week —
His stomach turned. . . . Two dollars fine, — or five!
If Minnie wouldn't give him hell, for sure!

Always yelling about the poor old Ford,
Bawling him out about the ninety dollars
He had put into it — the only time
He ever spent a cent upon himself.
Didn't she get all the four hundred over
From what Fred left him? Always nag, nag, nag . . .

What was it all about, this crazy world?
What was there in it? He turned the warping wheels
In the direction of his flat. . . . But no,
Not yet! He straightened them. . . . Not till his courage
Could find some reinforcement. . . . Say a slug
Of Dooley's gin. That might just help a little! . . .

But would it help? Could anything? Despair
Waxed as he threaded dismal, brooding streets
Along the water-front. A block from Dooley's
He shook his head. That rotten gin . . . his head
Would only grow more muddled. . . . Minnie would smell
His breath. . . . He passed the door of Dooley's joint,
Quickly. His eye was caught by the greasy glow
Of the river, beyond. The water seemed to flow
Little by little, into and through his mind.
Water over his head, into his throat,
Choking and agonizing at the first,
But bringing at last an end to hopeless struggle,
Unsuccess without end, insult and nagging. . . .

" Why the hell not? ", he mumbled, swinging the car
Out upon Riverside Drive, " Up above Dyckman,
Where there ain't nobody buttin' in to stop me —
Why the hell not? "

                              He pulled at the throttle-lever.
The streets flashed faster. " I'll do it — I'll do it! ", he
    crooned. . . .

A large car lumbered smoothly ahead of him.
He tried to pass. The driver grinned back slowly,

Increasing speed, swerving to leftward, also.
It was a moderate-priced American car,
New and shining, Saunders perceived with rage.
He dropped behind, then shot suddenly forward
Seeking to pass upon the right. The driver
Guffawed, accelerated, squeezed ahead.

And now, Saunders perceived an open stretch
Of boulevard before him. Frantic skill
Came to his aid. In a continuous howl
He shrilled his horn; he clawed the throttle wide.
A racing machine-gun, Lena made her bid. . . .

Saunders flashed a glare at the grinning face.
" You lousy ape! ", he screamed, " You lousy ape! "
Lena pulled past. " Say, who the goddam hell
You think you are, anyways? Own the road?
You lousy ape! I'll show you! " . . . Lena leapt,
Increasing her advantage over the lordly,
Infuriating patrician of the road.
Three blocks he sped, flinging over his shoulder
These and some kindred comments. Then he noticed
His rival turning up an angled street,
Defeated, obviously. . . .

                        And now he slowed.
A glow was in his cheeks. A little song
Hummed in his ears, taking its rowdy tempo
From the quick, happy beating of his heart.

Minnie? Oh, let her yell her doggone head off! . . .
And wait till he told Fleming about it tomorrow!

Gees! Would Fleming laugh! . . . And the gang at
    Dooley's! . . .

The story was beginning to form words:
" There he was, the lousy, dirty ape!
Sure, a Rolls Royce! Gee, the biggest speedster
I ever seen! But good old Lena — say!
Did she sail by it! Sixty-three, no kiddin'!
So then I tell him, ' Think you own the road,
You lousy ape? ' . . . How's zat? So then he says. . . ."

Grinning broadly, he whirled into a turn,
Heading for home and Minnie. . . .

Come, let me love you! This is a new Spring
  Filled with soft moons, insinuating fogs,
  The high, erotic murmur of the frogs,
The pungent earth-smell — oh, quite everything
That urges lips to lips, and breast to breast.
  Come, yield to me your fragrant loveliness,
  And we may find, in one dark, swift caress
A rhythm, and a beauty, and a rest
From the world's carping torments. . . . Why, who knows?
  Perhaps in that ecstatic harmony
  We might find Truth a moment! We might be
Something as true and lasting as a rose! . . .

You will not mind if, in my heart, there stay
The ghosts of many another searching May?

Kennedy was a top-sergeant in the War,
Wounded three times. He drives a truck, these days.
I meet him at American Legion meetings.
He talks with me, sometimes. The other night
He said, " Say, Loot. I got a story for you.
Maybe you can figger the answer out,
And write it up, and cop a piece of jack.
Remember we was talkin' about heroes
And cowards, and what makes 'em . . . all that hooey?
Well — look."

            He held a frayed newspaper clipping,
Dotted with rust-like spots. " Don't read it yet.
It's from ' The Stars and Stripes ' — you know, the paper, —
August the third, nineteen hundred and eighteen.
Them brown spots there is blood. . . .

                  Now, here's the dope.
It's by a ape, name of Mosely. He wrote it.
He was the dumbest private in my comp'ny.
What he knowed about soldierin' in the first place
Was a single-O with the edges off. And what
Anybody could seem to ever learn him,
You could write very big on a gnat's eyebrow,
And still have room enough for the Lord's Prayer.

232

" Everybody would ride him somethin' fierce.
First they called him Alice, for bein' so sweet,
Though big and strong. And then they called him Dopey,
Because he acted like he was full of hop.
I felt kinda sorry for him, but what can you do
With a sap that can't stand rifle-practice, even,
And every time he goes to bayonet-drill,
He gives one look at the sergeant stickin' the dummy,
And turns as green as a catfish two days dead,
And shoots his cookies, and has to go on sick-call?
And the worst yet, some of the boys found out
He was a poet. You know, writin' po'try.

" It seemed the second draft had come along,
And yanked him out of some lousy little joint
That printed greetin' cards — ' To My Sick Friend,'
And ' Happy Birthday,' and all that kind of junk —
Wise-cracks and verses. He didn't write 'em, see?
He was only a clerk, in the business end.
But what he was hopin' for, he'd get to writin'.
So he would practice every chancet he got.

" He was still practicin' on the sly, in the army,
For when the war would finish. After supper
Creepin' off, writin' away till ' Lights out.'
Even when we got over there, he wouldn't
Go with the guys and lap up that van rooge.
Not him. Scribblin' away, scribblin' away. . . .

" So one night old Fat Harper snitched a lot
Of Dopey's scribblin's right out of his pack.
Boy! If you could of read it! And the prize,

233

It was a thing, name of 'Mother o' Mine' —
'Mother o' mine, with your silver hair divine' —
That's how it started out — get the idear?

"The company made a marchin' song out of it.
Even goin' up to the front, whenever
It wasn't dangerous to make a noise,
They'd howl and yell it — never got tired of it.
Dopey wouldn't get sore enough to scrap
Even at that. He'd just pretend he liked it.

"Well, all of a sudden, somethin' happened to him.
Harper came runnin' up to me one day.
He had a copy of 'The Stars and Stripes.'
It had a pome in it. The pome was signed,
'Philip Mosely, private, 103rd. Inf.'

"I took it to the Old Man. He went to college.
He says it was a very swell piece of work.
Then I had Mosely front and center. I says,
'Did you write that there?' He says, 'Yes, I did.'
'That's all,' I says. I couldn't make it out.
It wasn't the kind of pome I really like.
It was so soft and girly — know what I mean?
But that was the way that Dopey was hisself.
And I could see the pome was all Okay.

"So here's what happened to him. Right away
He started goin' around like a different guy.
He stuck his chin in the air, and furthermore,
He started bein' a whole lot better soldier.
He didn't talk to nobody at all.

But he got neat, and when we had inspections
They didn't bawl him out hardly at all.
They didn't have to. He was one changed guy. . . .

" Well, we went up to the front in about a month,
And Dopey, he got killed, first crack in the box.

" This is the way it was: I made a call
For volunteers to go on a night patrol.
And Dopey was the first one that spoke up.
You could of knocked me down with a Chevrolet.
' What? You?,' I says, ' Say, you know what you're doin'?
You're puttin' in to join the Suicide Club.'
He stands there with his face all tight and funny.
' Sure. I'm a poet,' he says, ' I'll show you bastards.'
Can y'imagine him usin' such a word?

" So we run into some Heinies right away,
And he got two of 'em, just as they was startin'
To knock me off. So then another one
Sticks him right through the guts. So he kicks in.
And I crawls back. . . .

                        But just as I was goin',
He manages to reach in his shirt pocket,
And pulls me out this clippin'. ' Well, I showed you! ',
He says, and give it to me. Then he kicks in.

" So this is it. Give it back when you read it."
I read the verse. " Why — look here — ," I began.
But I was halted by what he said next.

"You know — it's sort of wonderful!", he said,
"I mean — what it did to that bozo. He's a sissy,
Also a crummy. Then he writes a pome,
And gets it published. And it's reely good.
It makes a new man of him — makes a hero
Out of a punk, and all account a verse
That sounds just like a girl. It's like he growed
A soul, ain't it? That's why I always keep it
Right in my pocket-book. It's — like you'd say
A inspiration, maybe — know what I mean?"

"It's a great poem," I said, handing it back,
"And I know what you mean about inspiration."

I never shall finish the sentence I began.
Why should I puzzle and confuse Kennedy
As, reading the poem, I'm puzzled and confused?
It is a lovely poem. It begins:

            "I will be the gladdest thing
                Under the sun.
            I will touch a hundred flowers,
                And not pick one. . . ."

It first appeared in a popular magazine,
Some time in 1915 or 1916,
Signed with the name, "Edna St. Vincent Millay". . . .

" You got a bargain, Mister," said Cap'n Adams,
Running an eye with warm appreciation
Over the sweet lines of the schooner-model,
" Yes sir. Ain't a better man at carvin' 'em
Than Holloway. Not in the hull o' Nantucket.
That's right, now ain't it, Holloway? "

                                     A grunt
From the white-haired ex-whaler was the answer,
And a brief mutter, " So they used to say."
" So I say, now," I agreed, with heartiness,
" I tell you, Mr. Holloway, you're an artist! "

" Thisn's a good rig," Holloway admitted,
" But I ain't been a artist only once.
I was a artist that time, wa'n't I, Adams? "

" I'm jiggered if you wa'n't," the Captain chuckled,
" He done a piece of carvin' one time, Mister,
Your eyes 'd popped clear out of your head to see it.
It was a masterpiece, that's what it was.
' Holloway's Masterpiece ' — that's what they called it.
Every whaler on the seas wanted it.
Took you nigh on a year to make it, didn't it? "

" Two year and two months! Get your figgers right! "
Corrected the old man, indignantly,
" And she was a beauty, though I say it as shouldn't! "

He settled down upon the rickety chair,
Puffed on his pipe, and fixed me with his eye.
" It's only a thing like love," he solemnly said,
" Can make a artist out of a plain carver.
I had it bad, I did. I promised Laura
The finest weddin'-present in the world.
It was the night I got engaged to her.
She begged and teased me to tell her what 'twould be,
But I just wouldn't tell. ' Why should I spile
Your weddin' gift by talkin'? ' — so I says,
Lookin' deep down into them pretty eyes
As blue as the water around the Caribbean;
And then I kissed both of them cranberry-cheeks,
And put out for my ship.

" 'Twas all of eight months before I could find a piece
Of whalebone big enough and fine enough.
Yes, whalebone! Now you understand the job
I set myself, and what a beauty it was
When I was through. O' course I couldn't give
All of my time to carvin' " — he smiled grimly —
" They's a plaguey lot of chores for a hand to do
On a three-year whalin' v'y'ge. But every minute
I had to myself, I was at it. The other hands
Was allus makin' jokes at me, at fust.
' What in tunket's Holloway up to now? '
They'd say, ' Makin' a teethin'-ring fer sharks? ' —
And sich-like feeble jokes. But when my ship
Begun to sort of take on shape, they stopped
Their larkin', and their eyes stuck out, I snum.
Out on deck, in the moonlight of the tropics,
I carved. Around the fo'c'stle stove, by the lantern,

When the wind was blowin' all git-out, I carved.
Summer, winter, spring and fall, I carved.
The months rolled by. Roundin' the Horn, I carved.
In the Pacific, amongst the South Sea Islands,
Blisterin' sun, or arctic ice, I carved.
Work, and whales, and carvin' — that's all I knowed.
Them, and blue eyes above cranberry cheeks,
Smilin' at me, 'way in the back of my mind.

" One day, Cap'n Sellers seen what I was doin'.
' Well, I be ding-donged if it ain't the image
Of this same Mary L! The spittin' image! ',
He says to me. And from that minute on
He kept at me to make me sell it to him.

" The other hands kept tellin' me, ' Look here,
You better let the old man have it. Why,
You'll get a mint of money if you do.'

" ' Shan't nuther! ', I'd say, ' I got a use for it.'

" ' But money's money,' they'd say.
                              ' And art is art! '
I'd answer. Then I'd quit the argymint.
' They's some things in the world that's too blame precious
To sell. And this is one! ' . . . They'd snort and whisper,
But they shut up. They knew that I was sot.

" It come along the end of the second year.
I was commencin' to fit the tackle on her.
That riggin' took a pile of workin', Mister.
But it wasn't nothin' only play to me.

239

" Pride in its beauty kept me goin' steady,
And love put extry skill into my hands.
It was a masterpiece, and no mistake.

" We met up with some other ships, of course,
And didn't them boys make a heap of miration,
Seein' my model. Dozens of 'em come
And tried to dicker with me. I just laughed.

" 'Twa'n't till two days before we come to harbor
That I could put the last licks onto her.
Then there she stood, straight and proud and true.
My Jeeminity! There ain't been such a piece
In the hull world, I jedge, afore or sence!

" That night, the Cap'n calls me in, and says,
' This leetle Mary L you took and made —
She *is* a dinger! Tell you what I'll do:
I'll give you a hundred dollars, cash in hand.'

" I was polite as could be, but I argied,
And made him understand. Part with the present
I'd cut out with my own hands for my Laura?
Sell the thing that had made a artist of me?
How could he think I'd do a thing like that?

" The news of my carvin' beat me into home.
It seems one of the ships we'd met out there
Had got in fust, and all the town was buzzin'
With talk about my whalebone masterpiece.

" Even before we got time to drop anchor,
A dinghy dropped alongside, and a man

240

Come up with old Bill Burke; it was a stranger,
A New York feller, looked like he was rich.
He says he represented a Museum,
And specialized in buyin' up ship-models,
And old Bill told him mine was such a beauty
He'd stayed there two days extry, just to see it.
He says he had to take the boat to the mainland
That left in the afternoon; but from the minute
He seen my model, he plumb forgot his hurry.
Talk! You never heard such a heap of talk!
Arguin' and persuadin', and strokin' it,
And danglin' rolls of bills in front of me.

"He started at a hunderd-fifty dollars,
And by the time we was ready to go ashore,
He was offerin' three hunderd. 'No, no, no!',
Was all I answered. And he grabbed my arm,
And made me come with him in old Bill's dinghy.

"All the way in, he stayed right at his talkin',
And just as we was layin' foot on land,
He says, 'Look here. You come up to the tavern
And have a little drink. It ain't so much
That I got any hopes of pryin' you loose
From the model, as it is I want to see it
As long as possible. It's shore a beauty!'

"'We-ell,' I answers, 'I might take a drink —
Just one. But as for buyin' my masterpiece,
You got the chance of a clean shirt in a fight.'

"We stepped on down the road, me carryin' it
Where all could see, and a big whoppin' crowd

Follerin' us, and pushin' to get near it.
So we set and had a nip, the New York feller
Raisin' his bid five dollars at a whack.

" I couldn't sing only one tune — ' No, no! '
And I was gettin' plenty tired of it.
I wanted to see my pretty little Laura,
And put the beautiful thing into her arms,
And watch her blue eyes shine, and her cheeks glow.

" Finely, I says, ' Well, Mister, take a look,
A last long look because I got to go.'

" He jumps up, and he yells, ' Four hundred fifty!
And that's the very highest bid I'll make! '

" I looks him up and down, and stands up straight,
And just as cool and ca'm as I am now,
I says, ' Mister, just let me tell you somethin'.
That's a big heap of money. It's the most
I ever had a chance to get my hands on.
But they's some things that ain't got any price,
They're sacred, and too precious to be bought.
This model, here — it was a labor of love! '

" And sayin' that, I marched right out the door,
And down the road to where my Laura lived.
She come a-runnin' crost the grass to meet me,
And throwed her arms around my neck, and then —
Well, it was just one of them things that never happens —
A time a dream you've had really comes true. . . .
And Lord! But she was crazy about her present! "

Holloway drew a deep breath, sighed, and spat.
He puffed upon his pipe in a deep silence.

" Gosh," he said finally, " What a run I had!
I dum near busted my neck ketchin' that feller
Just as he was gettin' on the boat."

" You — what? ", I asked.

                              " Why, yes. Like Laura said,
A set of table silver is a heap
Appropriater for a weddin'-gift,
And practicaller, too. . . . Yep, that's the kind
Of wife that Laura always was — real sweet,
And practical. . . . Well, look at how she put it:
Masterpieces belongs to the human race,
And she'd be selfish and ondutiful
By keepin' it out of the museum
Where all could get a pleasure out of seein' it.
After all, I'd had the glory of creatin',
And knowin' what I done was real, true art,
Which it's the artist's biggest reward, now ain't it?

" We got a mighty beautiful silver-set
For the six hundred Laura raised the man to. . . ."

I saw your beauty, and my pulse stopped still.
   Almost I spoke. But something seemed to say,
   " Some better moment, on some later day." —
But that was years ago. And never will
My moment come, I know. . . . And I am glad.
   That You I saw still kindles some desire;
   But Time has turned his damper on my fire —
(And you are not the You you were.) Ah, had
I spoken then! . . . But I am no longer young;
   And should I find you now still fresh and fair,
   My rashness has grown cold. I should not dare
Chance the rebuff. And I should hold my tongue. . . .

The energy involved is happier spent
On dining — and the result as permanent.

So look, Uncle Frank — it's this way, don't you see?
Everybody was always talkin' to me
How I should take the kid to Hollywood.
They sent me clippin's from the magazines,
And stories from the papers, all about
The life of ease them movie kiddies led.
And 'Look at Laddie Boy — just look at him.
Look at them big brown eyes!', they'd keep on sayin',
'And that there smile, so sad but also gay-like —
He's a dead ringer for Davey Lee and Coogan,
The both of 'em — and still he's different, too.'

My Laddie is, all right. Wait till you see him.
A reg'lar doll, and yet he's a hunderd per cent
Real boy — mischievous, know what I mean?
But the winnin' ways he's got, you can't have the heart
To stay sore at him for more'n a coupla minutes.
He's got a personality, that's it.
He was just born for the movies, like they said.

But where could we get the money to take him West?
There I was, breakin' my backbone washin',
And George, the dirty louse, boozin' away,
Drinkin' his wages up, and graftin' mine,
And beatin' me most the time, and always swearin'
He'd kill me if I ever took a sneak.

He meant it, too. And all the time, me knowin'
That Laddie was bein' robbed of a sure chance
For fame and fortune, and a life of ease. . . .

So all the time I read the movie-news,
And thought and schemed. And also all the time
I was keepin' up the insurance premiums
On George. Two dollars a month I had to pay.
It was for seven hundred. So one night
George come home after bein' away a week,
And he was worst soused than I ever seen him.
And so he knocked me down, and then he seen Laddie,
And Laddie was cryin' and sayin', 'Don't you dast
To hit my Ma!' . . . So George, he just hauled off
And hit my Laddie right smack in the face,
And knocked him all the way acrost the room. . . .
I thought for a coupla minutes he was killed. . . .

Well, George passed out in a while, and slept two hours.
Then he waked up, and started in to yell. . . .
He had the D. T.'s . . . So the doctor says
"Don't let that man get hold of another drink,
He's got the alcoholic poisonin',
And if he drinks another drop right now,
He'll die as sure as sure" . . .

                    And so I set
Thinkin' all night about the dirty brute,
And how he had hit me, and especially Laddie,
And prob'ly some time soon he might kill Laddie
If he got on another terrible drunk.

246

So George come to, and started yellin' for licker.
So I remember what the doctor said,
And I found some rotten whiskey George had hid
In the clothes closet, and I give it to him.
So George died. . . .

So then I took my Laddie to Hollywood,
And it was like a dream, the way it worked.
One of them castin' directors put me in touch
With a man name Eppstein, was a actor's agent.
Eppstein, he made a contract about Laddie,
That he should get him jobs, and what I promised,
I should give Eppstein ten per cent, three years. . . .

So right away, the baby gets a test,
And then he gets a little job in a picture.
There was three other boys, and a little girl;
But Laddie made a monkey out of them.
He worked three days, for fifteen dollars a day,
And even said some words, and they was crazy
About the way he looked, and how he talked. . . .

Then Eppstein, he comes to the house, and says,
" Didn't I say the kid's a natural?
Excelsior Films is crazy about him, see?
So, here's a contract that they're offerin'!
Two hunderd berries a week for the first year,
Three hunderd the second year, and then a option
For four — but I ain't givin' but two years.
Your Laddie Boy is off for fame and fortune,
And so are you, and so am I, because
Then we begin to shoot for the heavy dough! " . . .

I was so happy that I cried two hours.
At last — at last! All of my dreams come true!

Then I went to his room, and looked at him.
There he was, like a little combination
Angel and imp, and his lashes on his cheek,
So beautiful! And smilin' in his sleep.
You never seen such a boy in all your life —
Such a real, human boy! . . .

I sat there all night long, till it was day,
Tryin' to figure it out. . . . And so I found
They was a mornin' train to Omaha,
And the money he made those three days was enough
For a ticket — and somethin' over if you won't
Let us stay here. . . . And so we took the train. . . .

Leave us stay with you in Omaha, Uncle Frank!
I'm awful afraid to go back to Chicago —
I'm so afraid that Mr. Eppstein will find us!
He'll drag us to Hollywood! It goes without sayin'
He don't want to lose such a big money-maker
Like Laddie Boy would be. . . . And I signed the paper;
I'd have to let him use the kid — if he finds him.
I'll take care of the house, I'll do the washin',
I'll scrub the floors, I'll cook and wait on table —
Only help me to save my Laddie Boy!

If you could only see them movie kids!
If you could listen to 'em! Laddie's got
A right to grow up like a human boy,
And turn into a reg'lar human man!
Them little monkeys around the studios! . . .

You wouldn't believe that kids could be like them!
Fresh and stuck-up, and always braggin' and posin' —
Struttin' around and lookin' into the glass —
Just little punks, that'll grow to be big punks,
Or sissies! . . .

You seen the Singer's Midgets? That's what I mean.
Hard-boiled, and like they never was a child.

And the hours, workin' 'em way into the night,
Breakin' the rules and all the labor laws. . . .

To hell with fame — yes, and to hell with fortune!
I want my Laddie Boy, that's real, and gentle,
Sweet, and mischievous — and genuwine! . . .

Look, Uncle Frank — I'll go and bring him in.
You'll see what I been sayin' — oh, you'll see!
And, for God's sake, please help me! Never talk
About the movies — tell him he ain't good-lookin' —
Make out you think he'd be a rotten actor!
I'm goin' to! I got to! We can save him! . . .

Oh, Uncle Frank — God bless you! Oh, God bless you! . . .

Look — I'll go get him. . . .

I don't see how I can stand it any longer.
It ain't not only always bein' starved,
Not knowin' whether I'll work for weeks and weeks;
I could stand that some more. But it's the way
They treat you — I mean, the way they think about you.
Know what I mean? You ain't a human bein',
You're just a thing that maybe they can use.

It's the assistant directors — they're the ones.
They bawl you out, and shove you all around,
And all the time your name ain't Bill or Pete,
It's "You!" . . . Why, a man's got some pride, now ain't he?
I ast you, is it fair to talk the way
They do? Now, here's the sort of stuff I mean:

Last month I was workin' over to Paramount
In "Pearls and Girls." It was the party scene
Where Powell — that's Mr. De Puyster — gives a party.
So what does Artie Jacobsen come and yell?
"Listen," he yells, "Drink up your coca cola,
And eat them sandwiches like you enjoy 'em!
You're in the home of a rich millionaire!
And you're all havin' a goddam good time!"

Get it? Well, maybe that ain't it exactly.
But here's another time, in "The King's Revenge,"

That was the niftiest costume I ever had.
A full dress suit, and a ribbon over my chest,
And even one of them English monicles.
It sure was one swell set. So there we was,
At the King's court, and I looked very good.
They got me in two close-ups, with the king.
Well, after I done my big scene, where I talked
To the Prime Minister — I had two whole lines —
I was just standin' there, thinkin' about it,
You know, about it bein' only luck,
The way one guy is born to be a king,
And others never get no breaks, and how
Maybe if my old man was somebody else
I could of been goin' to royal courts,
And from the pitchers I seen of the real royals,
I looked a damn sight better than most of 'em —
Why, Lubitsch, he says " Cut," and not two seconds
After, this Lee, he shoots his face off loud,
And knocks the ideas right out of my head,
And there I am, only an extra-man.
" That's all! " he says, " Snap out of it, you bums!
All youse ambassadors turn in your wardrobe! "

Oh, well — maybe I'm sensitive, like.
But they won't let you have a single dream,
Or think you're anything. . . . Take just last week.
I knowed they was goin' to be a call for guys
That can grow a garden — that means raise a beard.
And if there's one thing I can do, it's that.
Less'n ten days is all I ever need
To get a muff that covers the whole chin.
So I go over and hang around the window,

251

And I need dough, you see, but still I'm sure
They can remember what swell work I do —
They ain't no extra had a better record —

And I was thinkin' what a really grand
Art these here movies is, after all, see?
And how I'm really gettin' somewheres, now.

Didn't that bird assistin' Wallace run
Into the castin' office, and yell out,
Not tryin' to be funny or anything,
Pointin' to all us guys that had growed beards,
" Ten of them airedales tomorrow, nine o'clock! "

Airedales! . . .

Life of the Party

(Soliloquy)

Just six years ago tonight it was —
Not a hunderd and six, just six . . . that's all it was —
The night me and Dan announced we was engaged.
I was so happy, it was like bein' drunk!
Dan was so funny! Everybody said
I sure was lucky to get such a funny husband.
" Always a laugh a minute. Don't you worry
About bein' blue, no matter what troubles come.
Old Dan'll laugh 'em off. Dan is a riot! "
That's what they said. . . . They didn't know the half.

That night he done a extra funny stunt.
Towards the end, when everybody was tired,
Why, Dan jumps up on top the dinin' table,
And scrouged down, waggin' his head from side to side,
And makin' groanin' noises, very loud,
Floppin' his arms, like flippers. . . . So then Bill,
His cousin, made like he was throwin' fish.
It was a reg'lar trained seal act, you see?
I laughed so hard I near had the hysterics.
That was the funny stunt I liked the best.
All that Dan ever had to do was make
That barkin' noise, and I would start in laughin'.

You know, when we got married three months later,
We was startin' down the aisle, under his breath

He made a little trained-seal squeak! Oh, my!
I got to gigglin' so I couldn't answer!
Wasn't that terrible? But it was cute.
It was my Dan, and I just loved him for it.
"We'll laugh our way along," I says to myself.

Of course, he had a plenty other tricks,
But that's the one that made me laugh the most.
It helped us through a lot, that bad first year.
Before Dan switched from the furniture factory
Into insurance, and got five more a week.
That made it so we got along heaps better,
Instead of really starvin' most the time.
The night he come home, yellin' that he had it,
He was the loudest seal you ever heard!

The next to loudest was a year from then
When he got five more raise. Oh, was we happy!
We figured it was all right to have a baby
Now that he got that raise . . . and so we did . . .
I guess I'd rather I didn't talk about it.
She didn't live. . . . But here's the point, of course:
When I come back from the hospital, so weak
I couldn't hardly talk above a whisper,
And sad, and all . . . why, Dan wouldn't let me cry.
He says, "Why, that's all right, old lady! Say,
Next time you'll have the swellest kid there is!"
So while I'm layin' watchin' on the bed,
He does enough stunts to be a vaudeville show,
And Bill comes over, and they start right in
Doin' the seal. . . . And I quit cryin' to oncet! . . .
So, when my Frankie come, why naturally

We had the seal act after the christenin' . . .
Frankie's the grandest boy in the whole world! . . .

But Dan didn't get any raise from that time on.
He worked real hard, but — I don't know what it was.
Either they didn't take him serious,
Or either he didn't know how to sell himself.
Anyways, it was the same old job and wages.
I scrimped and scraped and made things go, some ways.
Always hopin' he'd get a break real soon;
And always feelin' cheerful, account of Dan's jokes.

And then, six months ago, he got a hunch.
" You got to specialize! ", that's what he says.
" I'm goin' to study to be an actuary."
He started goin' to night school right away,
And studied very hard. . . . It cut me down
On what I had to spend, but still I knew
That if he got the job he had his heart on,
We'd be on Easy Street. Why, we could move
Into the cutest little flat I seen,
That's twice as big as this, and you can use
The roof, those summer nights when it's so hot!

You see, Fred Mears is goin' to get promoted
To be assistant manager. And so
That makes a vacancy for section boss —
Sixty a week, with ten men under him.
So with the studyin' Dan has been doin',
And because he been with the comp'ny all these years,
And everybody says he's such a good mixer,
Why, it's a cinch that Dan will get the place.
Besides, Fred is the oldest friend we got,

And recommended Dan to all the bosses.
So Dan works like a dog, makin' a showin'. . . .
So then — tonight he comes home whoopin' and hollerin'.
He grabs me by the waist, and dances with me.
He says Fred talked to him this afternoon,
And tells him J. B. says the job's all set —
(J. B.'s the manager) — and Dan's to get it! . . .

Dan waltzes me around till I was dizzy.
Then he gets on the 'phone and calls up people.
Astin' them over for a little party
To celebrate a secret. . . . so they come . . .
And now the other room is stuffed with friends
Havin' the gayest time, and Dan's the gayest.
It isn't much of a secret any longer.
He takes 'em off in corners, and he whispers.
And he's so happy . . . Oh, my God! So happy! . . .

I'm in the kitchen, dishin' out ice cream.
I'm happy, too. Then Fred comes walkin' in.
I take one look, and right away I know,
The way his face is, somethin's awful wrong.
" What is it, Fred? ", I says, tremblin' all over.
" You got to tell me quick. I got to know! "
So then he hems and haws, and finally tells.
At half past three, he went to Dan and told him
It was all set, and Dan would get his place.
But it must be a secret till tomorrow.
Well, Dan gets all excited, keepin' it in.
And, then to closin' time, he jumps around,
Laughin' and cuttin' up. Fred doesn't like it,
But hates to call him down. . . . If he only had of! . . .

So this is what Fred got through tellin' me:
J. B., the boss himself, is in the toilet,
Twenty minutes to five. And in comes Dan,
Jokin' and tellin' stories to five others.
Twenty minutes they stay there — twenty minutes
Until it's closin' time. Yes, twenty minutes
Times six — that's an hour and a half Dan robbed the firm of.
That's the way J. B. put it, talkin' to Fred.
He don't say anything to Dan — oh, no!
He just goes sneakin' off to Fred and tells him.
It's all Dan's fault. He brought the others there.
J. B. is roarin'. Fred can't say a word.
What makes him sorest is a lot of jokes
Pokin' fun at the bosses, includin' J. B. —
Not real mean jokes, just razzin' 'em a little.
It's a long story, and ends up with the words,
" And that, my dear, is how I met your grandma."

And now J. B. won't let Dan have the job!
J. B. says anybody who will trifle
And make a monkey out of theirself like that
Can't handle men. He can stay where he is,
But hasn't got the makin's for a leader. . . .
Oh, God — after these years — his one big chance
All gone to pieces — he'll never get another!
And just because he can't help bein' jolly. . . .
Oh, damn the fool . . . oh, the poor thing, poor thing! . . .

Look at him now, standin' up on the table,
And Bill pretendin' to throw fishes at him!
Look at the silly idiot, bein' a seal,
So happy . . . And pretty soon I got to tell him! . . .

257

I'm sick to my stomach, lookin' at him and listenin'
There he goes now, makin' the barkin' noises.
Everybody is laughin' fit to kill. . . .
God, I wisht we was dead . . . Poor little Dan. . . .
"Eeonk! Eeeonk!" . . . Poor little punk trained-seal! . . .

My Son Stands Alone

Suddenly, as you are clinging to my hands
With the accustomed clutch, I see a light
Blaze in your eyes. Your brows draw taut. Your feet
Patter for purchase. And your tongue thrusts earward.
Then valiantly you sway away from me. . . .

There is a weight pressing upon my heart.
One moment more, and you will cease to be
The funny, creeping, horizontal Something
Which never has won the Perpendicular
Save as some small attachment propped and guarded. . . .
Now . . . You will be a unit — and erect!

I thrust aside the fat solemnities
That crowd my thoughts; the pity and the longing
To spare you from the fight that you must make,
Ever and always, merely not to lose
The rudiments of the upright position —
The stumblings and the fallings and the bruises
That will be yours, until the ultimate hour
That crowns the victory of the Horizontal. . . .
But see! Your fingers lift, your body tilts
Backward — your arms are tiny, quivering wings —
The air rings with the gurgling, triumphant
Lilt of your laughter —
                    And you stand — alone!

259

I

Ancestors

Ancestors come and leer at me
　In most annoying places.
Against each glad impulse appears
　One of their dismal faces.

If passion seeks to take my heart
　(And other things) by storm,
Some snub-nosed ghost pipes up his creed
　Of sour Dutch Reform.

If some alluring lass suggests
　We might do thus and so,
Loud in my ears there roars forthwith
　A Puritanic " No! "

Do I resolve to spend some night
　All heedless of the morning?
A dour Scottish mug declaims
　In Presbyterian warning.

So, Huguenots and Lutherans
　Complete my soul's negation;
Each wild desire is cancelled by
　Protestant protestation.

Why couldn't I have Portuguese
  Within my racial blood?
They sin — confess — and sin again —
  (Or so I've understood.)

2
Zane Grey Please Write

All along the railroad track
The inhabitants wave back,
Showing teeth in cordial glee.
And this simply proves to me,

— Gazing at the wastes of sand
After seeing Kansas and
Iowa — that mankind's sense
Of nausea is not immense.

3
An Old Tune Reset for the Piccolo

Two loves I have that haunt me,
  And I must choose between.
And one of them's a gay love
  That laughs in eyes of green.
And one of them's the old love
  In placid pools of blue.
And one is emerald danger,
  And one is strong and true.

Now, if I keep the old love,
  I know that I shall be

Forever bathed in beauty,
    And clothed in sanity.
And I shall have the gladness
    Of arms that hold and hold,
Of strength and peace and candor,
    And tenderness untold.

Yet if I take the new love,
    I think that I shall go
Upon a path of splendor
    And ecstasy and woe,
Girded by flame and laughter,
    Winding through vales of fears,
Losing itself in questions
    Beside a gulf of tears. . . .

So I shall keep the old love,
    The love of peace and rest,
And that will be the real love,
    And that will be the best.
I daresay in the darkness
    Will sometimes come again
An echo of lost laughter,
    And temporary pain. . . .

4

Hail, California!

Beside your sea of meaningless, bright blue,
    Girdled with smug, pretentious, painted peaks,
    You sprawl, while the insipid sunshine leaks
Through the high-fogged complacency of you.

262

Expatriate Iowans hourly celebrate
    Your sawdust oranges, your paper roses,
    Your subdivided sands, your cultural poses,
And breed the spawn that thrives when morons mate.

Hail to your grinning insincerity!
    Hail to the emptiness of your women's eyes!
    Hail to your million frantic, antic lies!
Hail to your Weather, Hail! . . . Oh, God, to be

Waist-deep in slush, penniless, ague-cold,
But Eastern-circumstanced — and Eastern-souled!

5

A Little Girl Said:

(*For Emily Dickinson*)

" A sign's in the bird store,
    That I always read:
' Hartz Mountain Canaries —
    Singing Guaranteed! '

" Do you suppose
    When a bird gets bought
It tries to sing
    As well as it ought?

" Might it pretend
    It's no good any more,
So it can return
    To its friends in the store?

"Or would it work till it thinks
    Its throat will crack,
So the people won't hate it
    And send it back?

6

Somewhat Pompous Letter To My Child
On His Second Birthday

Two years old! And a Person, who thinks and dreams,
Laughs, is frightened, draws back, chatters, sings songs . . .
Gay, romping, shy . . . sensitive . . . sensitive . . .

Well, you have charm of body and of manner —
A " Winning Personality " — but something
Further, that dims my eyes, clutches my throat
With fear for you. Why must you have that Soul?
Why not be merely a healthy animal
Eating and frisking through the normal day?
Why must you share the sorrows of the world —
Weep when Bo-peep loses her silly sheep,
Whimper when pigeons do not get their crumbs,
Sob when " the man " must go without his dinner?

Oh, well . . . go on and be a poet, then.
But don't come yelping up to me some day,
Holding your heart, with your soul all black and blue. . . .

7

Middle-Aged

I knew that middle age would be
A losing of curiosity.
And how, and when, and why, and where —
I do not any longer care.
I plod a safe, habitual way,
Nor thrill to whisper " Ah, some day . . ."
But view with apprehensive eye
An unproductive bye-and-bye.
O! If I only had not lost
Desire to rush and see the frost
Dashing its colors on the leaves;
To smell the perfume of new sheaves;
To taste the richness of the mud;
To let the sunrise whip my blood! . . .
But I am past such pioneering.
Mildly amused or vaguely fearing,
I carry my small, smothered soul
Cautiously toward a tiresome goal,
And do not even wish to hear
If the same phoebes came back this year. . . .

✣ TRIAL BALANCE ✣

A SENTIMENTAL INVENTORY

". . . And this is all that is left of it! Only a moment; a moment of strength, of romance, of glamour — of youth! . . . A flick of sunshine upon a strange shore, the time to remember, the time for a sigh, and — good-bye — Night — Goodbye. . . .

". . . our weary eyes looking still, looking always, looking anxiously for something out of life, that while it is expected is already gone — has passed unseen, in a sigh, in a flash — together with the youth, with the strength, with the romance of illusions." —

YOUTH,
by Joseph Conrad

I am an egotist.
I cannot think in abstract terms, in terms
of life and art and love and literature
except as they affect me, or I them.
" *I* like this rose." . . . " This sunshine is too brash
for *me*." . . . " The third movement of Brahms' Second
to *me* is curved and soft and dainty and firm —
experimentally voluptuous
as the breasts of some young beauty at the court of a
    Louis." . . .

" The ground in Cézanne's landscapes seems to squirm
in agony, and looks as if it suffered
as *I* have suffered . . . on the day I quite decided
there definitely could not be a God." . . .
In any of which, I assume I cannot differ
by much from other men . . . but I must think so. . . .

Let me point out that when the gigantic rhythms
of higher mathematics spread their glories
before my comprehension, and I felt
for meanings of some phrase such as " light-years,"
heard the stars numbered,
learned they had colors,
measured their distances,
I became drunk with self-appreciation,

knowing myself a dealer in rhythms, too,
therefore important in the infinite scheme
of infinite rhythms, nicknamed a universe —
a very God myself, in a puny way. . . .
And then, since worlds and kings, eras and gods
might be, in reason, only electrical
discharges, equally silly in time and space,
why . . . I, myself . . .

My life has reached a Certain Point.
I sit back and examine it.
I shall make an inventory,
a spiritual bookkeeping,
a listing of soul-assets.
I must take stock.
For see, my years are thirty-eight.
Twice thirty-eight makes . . .
And your old Bible taunts you
with that three-score-and-ten, reminding you
that if by chance you might crawl past the mark . . .
Then, there are, among the myriad debits,
these all-too-present liabilities,
the swelling paunch, the dimming eyes,
the skull-pains after excesses,
the rustiness in elbows, the . . .
But it were an endless task
to cover the losing side.
What have I gained?
What assets may I list?
I must begin:

Item: Astronomy . . . reaction noted.
Item: Cosmology . . . reaction listed.
Items . . .

To run free,
to gulp the breeze,
to bite the grass,
to fall from trees,
to be impressed
with a little money,
to laugh because
there's nothing funny,
to spend hours
throwing stones,
to know nothing
about bones,
to work magic
with knives and strings,
to eat strange
sickening things,
to be proud
of mere strength,
to keep elders
at arms'-length,
to disobey
from sheer joy —
such are duties
of a boy.

So at noon I said to Bill, "Let's beat it, hey?"
He nodded, then he frowned. "But — wait a sec —
there's Latin and algebra this aft," he said.
"Oh, hair on Latin, and fuzz on algebra!
Right after lunch, you duck out the back window.
I got my bike hid under a little bush."

We pedaled through the crystal October sunlight,
whooping and yodeling . . . at Diamond Lake
we pooled the residue of our spending-money,
purchased five strips of bacon, a loaf of bread,
some butter, a small cheap frying-pan, and a cake
of chocolate, and hired a rickety rowboat. . . .

There was a certain bay among the cattails
hidden behind Goose Island. With blistered hands
I dropped a line, baited with bacon-fat,
into the ruffling mirror. Bill brought forth
three cigarettes, sneaked from his father's desk.
We saved one. . . . I caught seven fair-sized perch,
two sunfish, and a three-pound pickerel.
Bill wouldn't fish. He curled up in the stern,
and made up yarns about the cotton clouds.
Ripe wild crabapples were pungent on the breeze. . . .

When the mauve sunset fell into the riot
of crimson in the trees, I scaled the fish,
while Bill erected a small, chuckling fire. . . .
Later, we lay in the gloom, and watched the flames,
grunting with plenty, puffing the frayed ends
of cigarette halves, while we made bad guesses

at all those problems, theological
and biological. . . .

As we rode homeward, under the grinning stars,
debating which of our tales would best go down
with parents, we came upon Ken Allenby,
the enemy . . . only two weeks before,
he had knocked me down, and made me swallow dirt,
disgracing me before a crowd of girls.

I jumped from my bike at once, and ran straight at him.
Bill was the referee, and interfered
whenever Ken tried any of his tricks —
butting or using thumbnails — for twenty minutes
of mauling, and fists thudding. . . . At the end,
Ken limped along the silent street, cursing me,
and flinging back loud promises of vengeance
between his sobs. . . . I laughed from bleeding lips,
and crowed victorious taunts. . . .

My father listened gravely to my brief
and undefiant explanation: " Oh,
I went out fishing, and then I had a fight."

He nodded. " Very well. You will stay home
next Friday night and Saturday afternoon.
Also, I'll take away this week's allowance."

That was a bargain. I felt the price was fair. . . .
As I scrouged down between the fragrant sheets,
I laughed aloud, splitting my lips again.
I kept on laughing, till something soft and black
whiffed out the spot of starlight on the bedpost. . . .

He was my friend. We ran and walked
and loved and hoped and played and talked.
Each was the complement of the other.
He was my friend, and more than brother.

I met him, several days ago,
after fifteen years or so.

Our conversation caught a thread
or two of interests long dead.
And he was bald and plump with power,
and I was thin and quick and sour.

He was a bore, and I a bore.
I do not make friends any more.

" Young gentlemen, you are now going out into — "
Lord! The heat, and the slippery, pallid faces
of relatives, classmates, professors, swimming through
the June stench of the gym . . . twenty-two cases
of beer last night! That's what I call a spread! . . .
" Buzz-buzz, gobble-gobble, completed your education,
go out prepared for the grim fight ahead,
armed with ideals and guff and blah . . . the nation — "
I'll get four dollars for the cap and gown —
they cost eleven . . . yes, I might as well
work in the bank, to start with . . . still, a town
so small . . . insurance must be easy to sell . . .
I'll grab that little Alice tonight, and kiss her . . .
so soft and round . . . thank God, at last the noise
of Prexy's blather stops . . . I'll really miss her . . .
" Oh, Alma Mater, we still will be thy boys. . . ."

Hours later, in the lilac-cloyed dusk,
we sat upon the porch of the fraternity house,
we four, watching the little lights of houses
exploding noiselessly, one by one, in the valley.
We spoke not at all.
I was thinking of myself,
as I first mounted this hill,
a gangling colt,
and of how I was now mature,
a man of almost-twenty-one;
of athletic teams unachieved;
of " college spirit ";
of " brotherhood," and of the melancholy
of leaving youth behind. . . .

The mists began
their unhurried march up from the Oriskany.
With an excellent miming of spontaneity
Alice and I went through the formula
of wandering accidentally away from Jim and Edith.

In the scented seclusion of the old graveyard
her lips trembled against mine
almost with enough fervor to set up
a vague gnawing in my mind
for having hesitated two whole months
before daring this tentative amorous routine.

It did not occur to me that she was expecting
demonstrations possibly more sophisticated
than a number of fumblings and kisses,
sundry acknowledgments of her " sweetness,"
and vows to write her often.
I recall being vaguely surprised
at a certain snappishness with which she greeted
my insistence that we should rejoin the others.
I believe I must have attributed the coldness
with which she said farewell
to remorse at having lowered
her maidenly barriers even to that extent.
But my ego had been sufficiently enhanced.
I had accomplished all my intentions.
I had drawn two lines
under a balance.
That was that. . . .

At midnight, stretched out upon old blankets
under the murmuring blackness of the elms,
Jim and I broke at last through the walls
of conventional diffidence and adolescent shyness.
At last I could thank him for how,
that sophomore year of weltschmerz,
he had often locked me in with my books,
and beaten me, to make me study,
and sweated with me,
averting scholastic disasters. . . .
He coughed his embarrassed cough,
and thanked me for Keats and Shelley,
Conrad and Shaw. . . .
I understood. . . .

So, while the procession of planets
swung heavily overhead, progressed
the solemn recital of our friendship.
" Do you remember the day — "
" Remember the night — "

Our talk grew pompous with boast and promise.
Now, we were setting forth
to tear our fortunes from the teeth
of a fierce but to-be-conquered world.
We would emblazon our names
high upon the walls of Time,
inspired always, in our battle,
by the holiness of the noblest,
the deepest passion, Friendship! . . .

I reached out into the darkness, and gripped his hand,
that great, firm, hairy hand, so male, so sure,

and strength flowed into me, as from a fountain —
strength, and a savage stream of exaltation. . . .

My friend! My friend!
My friend! . . .

Young love never thinks;
only feels; fears; burns;
worships; lusts; hopes; slinks;
smashes; lifts; stabs; yearns. . . .
After, perhaps,
laughter . . . perhaps . . .

And so, this night, she said, " Yes, please come over.
Everyone else is gone. I'm all alone
for the night. Come after dinner. I'm feeling rather
seedy. I want to talk. Or, you could read."

She opened the door herself. " The servants have gone
to the country with Aunt Maud and Uncle Henry.
They're opening up the house for Spring. Oh, my — "
she yawned and smiled, " I just begged off . . . so lazy. . . .
Spring fever's bad! " . . . She went back to the bed,
and propped her ash-blond curls on baby-pillows.
And I looked at the young, strong, slender body
through the white chiffon vapor, and leaned upon
a chair, to steady against the dizziness,
and did not try to speak from a dry mouth,
while she smiled lazily up, her amber eyes
veiled by long, lacy lashes. . . . " Sit there," she said,
" and tell me pretty stories " . . . and I sat,
but all my love was pushing against my teeth,
and I had promised to say no more about it;
I clenched them tight. She understood, and, pitying,
but nevertheless determined, closed her eyes,
waiting in languid, easy patience.

Two minutes or more I held my tortured silence,
sick with my plight's insolubility.

(Nothing had changed, essentially, during the year
of insistent slavery to this obsession.
" Oh, please don't fall in love with me! " she had begged,
when, after one dancing-party and one dinner,
she had read what all my bearing said too plainly.

"I know I'll never love you — that way — never!
It's no use arguing! It's no use trying!
To me, it would happen at once, the very first instant —
there wouldn't be any question! It didn't happen,
and now it never will! I'm cruel! I'll hurt you!
Forget you ever saw me! . . . I like you so much,
I wish I could love you — but I know I can't!" . . .
Because I was twenty-five, and now at last
something had swept into me, and I was helpless,
will-less, obsessed . . . I could only choke, and mutter,
"I'll make you love me! I'm not afraid — I'll make you!"
And because she was nineteen, I thought I could. . . .
The months had trooped past, and intimacy had grown;
I had given her worship, and a puppy-love
complex with books and music and some flashes
of adult understanding. In response,
she loved me — as a friend, as a companion,
but not that way — no, never once "that way.")

Grimly, I closed my senses, started chatting
of persons seen, of places. Presently
a desperate glibness aided: I talked well.
Fresh, flavorous words came pouring. I found humor.
She laughed, she was at ease; a tenderness
chimed in her voice. I was charming her, as seldom
in all the hours of my frantic wooing. . . .

The heavy April languor of the night
stole in, and dropped a subtle hand upon her,
so that her breath came slow, her smile was slow,
she answered slowly, looking at me deeply
with depthless eyes, half closed. And, in a while,

282

she said, " Darling, that book you made me read
last year — I loved that story so. You know,
the first one, ' Youth.' I have a sort of feeling
this is a special moment. You must read it.
I love your voice. I want to hear you read it."

I turned out all the lights, saving the one
to read by. With the corner of my glance
I was incessantly aware of rounded
pink flesh above the chiffon, fallen open.
But, because I was twenty-five, and the silver words
sang of themselves their pæan of being young,
the whole became a song which I was living,
with three refrains, weaving and interweaving;
immortal triumph, immortal tragedy;
" Ah, Youth! " . . . " Judea, London — Do or Die! "
(She is my love, my glory.) . . . " Pass the bottle! " . . .
Huskily I gasped out the ending words,
shut up the book, and stood beside the bed.
It was only then I dared look straight at her.

Through tears of self-pity and drama and defeat
I saw tears clinging lightly in her lashes,
and she was smiling with half-open lips,
and lifting out her hands, slowly, so slowly.

Her fingers pressed against my throbbing cheeks,
pulling my forehead down to her bared shoulder.
Aroma, of her body, and some perfume,
pierced the remotest fibers of my desire;
red globes of light shot through an indigo space
back of my eyes. . . . Then, through the crescendo roaring

283

within my tumbling brain, disjointed phrases
cried, " You are my love! My love, my God, my Youth!
You are all goodness, all faith, all purity! " . . .

Presently, as from very far away,
I heard a trembling whisper, incredible:
" Take me, darling! Take me — take me now!
This is your moment! It may not come again,
ever! . . . I know it will not come again! " . . .

Back through the years, I perceive a Noble Youth
straighten, bend quickly, place a solemn kiss
upon her forehead, pace to the doorway, turn,
say with firm reverence, " Good night, dearest love!
Will you remember always that some spell
once fooled you — and I wouldn't take advantage? "

Then, down the quiet streets, on his High Horse,
Noble Youth galloped, breathless and elated. . . .

It takes two to catch a dream.
    You must both be aware
well before, where it lies
    warily hidden. Dreams scare
easily. And you must go
    with your nets fashioned of
hope and determination,
    patience and love. . . .
Then, when you see it clear,
    do not fumble or hesitate;
deftly make your cast; the next
    moment may be too late.
Work with great gentleness,
    not to harm the gold that clings
to its feathers, nor the frail
    splendor of its wings.
Hold it close to your heart
    while you count three;
look at it intently;
    then set it free.
Fools may advise caging it
    or stuffing it. . . . Never!
Follow this plan, and have
    a nice dream forever. . . .

Was I really in love, really in love at last?
Well, it began to look it. . . . The May sun cast
yellow heat on the honeysuckle and boxwood hedges,
and stewed from them such a fragrance! . . . and down
        among the sedges
the Potomac peeked blue-eyed, laughing glances, and
I felt suddenly complete peace, and that the clasp of your
        hand
was necessary to me forever . . . meanwhile, you smiled,
and told me I was an interesting man, and a dear child.

Then we went into Mount Vernon, and appreciated
the luxurious taste of the rooms, and were charmed by the set
of whalebone teeth, and said that Washington must have
        hated
his work and his fellows, because these hurt his gums . . .
and expressed heartfelt regret
that we could not have met him; and agreed
that history did him foul injustice in taking no heed
of his humanness, manufacturing a star-spangled Babbitt,
while the real man must have been fine, cross, debonair,
impatient, sophisticated, possessing every habit
antipathetic to volsteads and chambers of commerce, and a
        flair
for living gone forever from these shores . . . and the day
        spun on,
and we liked each other increasingly . . . and when we had
        gone
out into the Virginia afterglow, we made a decision
to set forth on a hunt together, chasing a vision. . . .

VII

The drab, the gray,
The shadows fall away;
Only what you have loved shines through:
You are " dreaming true."

Wherefore
we peered through the fog of a July night,
leaning against the wet rail, my arm tight
about your shoulders . . . and Mrs. M., your chaperon,
a nice old thing, said, " There's Cherbourg! " . . .
and the fog-horn's moan
found its echo in my breast, and
" What? That? " I muttered through tight lips.
" It's going to be all right! " you whispered,
touching my mouth with your finger-tips.
" Yes, certainly, of course it is,"
I answered with the emphasis of doubt.
Then sailors began to scurry like beetles, and shout,
and it all seemed stupid and sordid,
and it began to rain,
and you pressed close against me, and
" It's going to be all right! " you said again.

But . . .

   Mass-jammed drenched gangplank . . . *douanier* forty-
minutes one small bottle of perfume not declared . . . shouts
roars mangled english mingled with mangled french . . .
estaminet closed . . . *cabinets* — comment omitted . . .
only train an *omnibus* sorry we canthelpit . . . no, zere ees
not a boat-trene — oui, in wan houaire, certainement . . .
dank waiting room stank . . . sky weeping forlorn hopeless
tears . . . brightbrightchaperonjokes from Mrs. M. . . .
from Mr. M., sneezes . . . from me, half-swallowed curses
. . . from you, little frightened pats. . . .

The train . . . third class only.

Compartement cinq,
contents, reading from left to right:
>Mrs. M., haggardly beaming,
>pointing out window at dripping nothing.
>Mr. M., sneezing.
>One peasant woman, stuffed into greasy rags,
>estimated weight, in toto, three hundred.
>One peasant son,
>equipped with dirt and running nose.
>One babe,
>sex indeterminate for the first ten minutes,
>complete with shrieks and colic.
>You.
>One beet-nosed gaffer, cargo wine.
>Two ducks and a pullet in a wooden cage.
>One old maid from Davenport, Iowa,
>nauseated.
>One lass, pink-cheeked, ballooned of bosom.
>Myself.

Odors:
>Garlic, stale wine, poultry, molars, sweat,
>french cigarettes, feet, exhalations,
>two indescribable,
>and two which shall be nameless.

Noises:
>Snores, rumbles, hiccoughs,
>murmurs in patois,
>train-wheels' ka-tick, ka-tick,
>whistles' pip-pip, squee-squee,

squalls, comfortings, refusals to move over,
chirps of encouragement (Mrs. M.),
sneezes (Mr. M.).

Hour
upon
hour.

At long last,
Squeeee! Pip-pip! Katick, ka-tick, ka t i ck.
Stop.

Drizzle splash where-the-goddamned-hell-is-the-rest-of-our-
       luggage
Porteurporteur! he says the taxi-fare is double this time of
       night . . .
what the triple-expletive of it? . . . why, John! . . . oh,
       shut up! . . .
oh! . . .

Mr. and Mrs. M. lost, thank God! . . . They'll find their
       way
somehow . . . fall into taxi, bags over and under . . . my-
       self taut
and furious . . . you speechless, hurt, lip-trembling . . .
       oui, m'sieu,
Hotel Nemo, Boulevard Raspail, bon! . . .

Quack-quack, quack-quack, lurch, hurl, slither,
quack-quack, skidding, quack-quack-quack,
jumbled, hideous quack-quack buildings
through the quack-quack slimy night,
furious silence, wounded silence,
quack-quack, quack-quack. . . .

A steel ribbon above the buildings,
rain pattering more thinly.
" Dear . . . that's the Boulevard des — "
" I don't give a damn if it's the Boulevard de Hell! " . . .

Silence.
Quack.

Suddenly
a crimson flush all over the sky,
and the rain turned off, as if a faucet shut.

I leaped to my feet, and pounded on the glass,
" Arretez! Cessez! Stop! "
The chauffeur slammed his brakes. We skidded three circles.
I seized your hand, I dragged you from the car.
We stood there, gaping about in a great arc.

Before us, a foolish river, and a bridge
with statues . . . on the left, a building, long
and low and smutted . . . a tower of spider-web . . .
a majestic arch . . . spread over it all, a burst
of purple, scarlet, gold and the heaving sun.

And . . . something in the air, of wetted dust,
blossoms and asphalt, petrol-vapor and women,
dung, and romance, and youth. . . .

(Backward, grope backward through fogs of sophistication!
Wipe from your lenses the flyspecks of the years!
" Trite and conventional " — hold the words unspoken!
Dinners atop the Butte, au Vieux Chalet,

incredible *langouste*, velvet Pouilly
served by Nini, a lecherous-eyed madonna;
whispering leaves of the Bois; the far-off band;
shrill shrieks of horror from delighted children
coagulated around the loud *guignol;*
Lapin Agile, so anxiously bohème;
snails like black teething-rings, at L'Escargot;
rose-window of Chartres, and towers of Carcassonne;
at Nimes, the *course de vache,* where I leaped to the ring,
and pulled the tail of the absurd, fierce cow;
Orange, the garnet Château-Neuf-du-Pape;
and that last night, when you stood by Louise's house,
and shot your voice to the trembling, fading stars,
over the verminous casements, " depuis le jour " . . .
Ah, me! How like a " Diary of My Trip! " . . .
Hush! Do not say again how, not long since,
Paris was grim and mercantile and thrifty,
booming and dull — with half the élan of Pittsburgh.
Stand with me this one moment, hand in hand,
giddy with youth, and boozy with romance.)

I seized your waist, and whirled into a dance
of leaps and pirouettes and bounds and yelps,
howling, with open lungs, " auprès de ma blonde."
The chauffeur stared, with sad, stuffed-olive eyes. . . .

Then you stopped giggling, and looked at me,
and smiled . . . slowly we kissed . . . and then we turned
and walked to our taxi, quiet as Cook's tourists,
clutching our dream. . . .

VIII

In the dark wine of your caress
I shall drink forgetfulness.

In the cool of your eyes
I shall be washed of lies.

Upon the warm white of your breast
I shall find rest.

Well. . . .
It is easy to say, " Yes, we will be married! " —
to say it glibly, loudly, gaily.
And then . . . to find that you are harried
by an army of troubles, doubling daily —
relatives armed with circumstantial
evidence proving that such as you
have neither character, nor financial
backing for *this* (and it all sounds true)
well. . . .
What with knowledge of all your failings,
fears and faults and lacks and ailings,
fled is the magic, faded the spell —
love's sweet song is a doggerel.

I stood on a tender, in the harbor of Hamilton,
which is situate on the island of Bermuda,
on a chilly, lowering morning of February.
The hour was eight o'clock. I had taken no breakfast —
unless a roll and several whisky-sodas
are rightfully a breakfast — and no sleep.
I strained my eyes for the thin wisp of smoke
which would be your ship . . . and waited. I was used
to waiting. Twenty months of shifting minds,
of longing, hating, loving, quarreling
and worshiping were coming to an end.
By God, they were! For better or for worse
we were resolved to put it to the test.

Even now, I was not entirely sure of you. . . .
Not even of myself . . . yet was I not? . . .
Thus, fearing still lest, at the ultimate moment . . .
I held my head, and waited for my love. . . .

A speck of soot upon the far horizon.
The speck enlarged. I hung upon the rail
and suddenly was violently sick.
The ship drew near. I dabbed my throbbing face,
and clenched my finger-nails into my palms.
The ship loomed black above. I squeezed my mouth
into a grin of fervent nonchalance.

I swallowed at my heart. I saw your eyes. . . .

It could have been, " It's a nice day, isn't it ? "
The words I blandly used were, " Hello, darling!
We're being married at six, in the cathedral."
Then, through the whirl of noises came your voice,
trembling a little, with a gay, quick laugh,
" All right! " . . .

What are the ingredients of a miracle?
What, for five weeks,
can lift two human hearts
into a state of radiant out-of-selfness,
foolish and beautiful,
intense and calm?
A large room, simply furnished . . .
a simple, white tray-ceiling . . .
a grizzled sea-captain,
adept at cribbage, yarning into the night
of years when ships had sails, and life had salt . . .
his ancient wife,
shedding about her a quavering sweetness . . .
bicycles, scorching down smooth white shell roads
which never a motor's hooting has profaned . . .

old wines from dim shops . . .
golf on the crinkled grass . . .
whisky-sodas and ritualistic teas . . .
the snowy coral, the cobalt sea . . .
the crisp " klop-klop " of horses toward midnight . . .
the bird that haunted the moonlight with its wail
of routine sorrow, " Dear, oh dear, oh dear! " . . .
the balm of rain . . . the balm of cedar-scent. . . .
But these were after. Now, we spent the day
gossiping, seeing places, making talk.
The dark drew down. I stopped at a small florist's
and loaded you with the white, subtle blooms
of freesia . . . ah, and it was Saint Valentine's Day.

The darkness swooped.
The cathedral . . . but, it seemed, a pair of negroes
had similar ideas, and had them first.
We must wait. Very well. To pull ourselves together
we repaired to a smelly pub across the way.
Three brandies quelled my panic. I believe
two sherries aided you . . . and suddenly
the consul said, " It's time! " . . . and so we ran
across the road, and were amused to see
the negro wedding-party, very formal
in evening clothes, faces invisible,
white shirts and dresses bodiless in the black. . . .

The gray, great walls . . . the emptiness . . . the ring
I had bought in Paris, nearly three years before . . .
the consul and vice-consul, and their wives
erect and solemn . . . the slow, stately words
of the Church of England service . . . and the white
of the freesias which, my love, you left in the pew. . . .

Quite sentimental and obvious, it seems.
We stalked down the aisle, striving to match our steps.
I saw the canon — not a bishop, a canon —
extremely pious, extremely serious,
and a phrase came flashing, to seal the marital bond
with the saving seal of laughter.
Into your ear — that dear, long-suffering ear
which has suffered the tawdry secrets of my heart —
I whispered eight quick, idiotic words:
"Hark! Hark! It is the canon's opening roar!" . . .

IX

Yes, the blame is ours.
It is we who invoked dark powers,
and out of the void brought you.
A scurvy trick, it is true.

Now you have been hurled
into a tinsel world,
try to make the best of it,
try to see the jest of it,

try to catch romance.
That is our only chance.
If there are moments when
life has a beauty, then

for this that we have done
forgive us, my son.

Pallid impersonality of walls,
harsh snowiness of linen,
hushed efficiency of nurses' voices,
the stench of ether. . . .

It's got to go right, this time!
If the first had only lived,
the little girl! . . .
It's got to go right, this time!
The nights I have found her, quietly weeping
because the small head
she had so long desired never pressed
upon her breast. . . .
It's got to go right, this time!
Inscrutable mystery of this craving,
this searing lust for motherhood!
Cigarette butts littering the room,
ashes griming the table, the chairs, the floor.
It's got to go right, this time,
Sweat gluing shirt to armpits —
oh, you're the one who's suffering,
are you, you fool?
but . . . if I should lose her . . .
nonsense! She'll come through again,
of course she will!
It's got to go right, this time,
got to go right!
Got to! . . .

" Congratulations! Both are fine!
Would you like to see him?

She's still asleep.
Come this way, if you please."

Infinite peace was upon her face.
Her eyelashes lay along her cheeks so calmly.
The beat of her breathing
was like the rise and fall of slow billows.

Upon her shoulder he lay.
He did not screech nor whimper.
I looked at his face.
It was not a wizened blob,
nor like that of some sour, apoplectic granny.
It was the face of a baby,
as one imagines the faces of babies,
if one approves of babies.

Something happened at once,
which caught my breath,
and caught my heart,
and bound me with a bond which never shall break
while there is breath in us:
he scowled.
You would have sworn
he was scowling directly at me,
his forehead furrowed
fiercely, accusingly.
"Hello," I said.
The furrow deepened.
And, in that moment, I was profoundly aware
of the debt I had incurred to him
for thrusting upon him

the dubious gift of life.
And, in that moment,
I took an oath to repay
as best I may.
Always I shall endeavor
to thrust into his hands
the little I have learned,
the much that I have felt,
the visions I have dimly seen,
the music I have heard,
all, all that has held loveliness
amid the blaring chaos. . . .

If he will not take —
still, I shall have offered. . . .

And, at the end,
perhaps he will be my friend.

X

Keep pretending;
keep lying;
keep stifling;
keep denying
everything your
heart is crying;
easier so;
quite secure;
it is empty;
it is pure;
daring can
only hurt you;
guard, oh guard
that precious virtue;
whip down passion;
hark to duty;
turn a frightened
back on beauty;
you can remember
all life long
that you did
nothing wrong.

They were two exiles in the land of oranges.
" Connais-tu le pays ou fleurit l'oranger? "
But that is another, wistful land.
Here is Nature bawdily flamboyant,
Humanity at the megaphone,
life one vast, blatant pageant.
Reticences? Niceties?
Mankind a playful, beaming moron,
yawping, gamboling,
sucking spiritual teeth,
belching with plenitude,
yelping self-satisfaction to the leering skies.

And because they were of another tradition,
easily abashed, hypersensitive, let them call it,
they drew toward one another.

To state it with baldness,
she was lonely, confused, disheartened,
and missed her husband, whom she loved,
and who was many miles distant,
while he mooned for his wife and child,
who were more miles and many months away.

The days galloped by,
and the sight of the other,
and the sound of the other,
became as food and drink and books to each.

But . . .

There were inhibitions, barriers
of bourgeois morality,

303

the Past, the Future,
What Would Be Best,
Oughts, Shoulds, Musts, Must Nots,
consciences, loyalties. . . .
And so . . . It did not happen.

Nothing happened
except a game.
The days quickened.
They played at their game.
Demurely, savagely,
daintily, fiercely,
laughingly, sadistically,
morosely, masochistically,
cautiously. . . .

Then . . . suddenly it was Spring.

Spring comes stealing to other lands
with a subtle, gentle smile on her lips,
and little flowers in her hands,
and little scents on her finger-tips.
Something whispers out of the earth
of tenderness . . . mystery . . . rebirth.

But here
Spring comes whooping and cavorting in,
a gin-inflamed, voluptuous wench,
flinging her charms at a dazzled world,
raping the startled soil.

Nevertheless,
Spring is Spring, even gone Hollywood.

That day
the girl announced with finality
and enough sorrow
that she would be going away
upon the morrow.

The man accepted the sentence,
glum with envy.

This, then, was their last evening together.
They motored into the city,
and dined charmingly where the tagliolini
reminded him of that place in Venice,
and she agreed that the scallopini alla marsala
brought back the Castello dei Cesari on the Tiber.
His forehead was drawn tight.
He was apparently extremely witty,
talking without cease.
She laughed continually,
half an octave higher than usual.

Presently they drove to his house,
and she stretched out upon a chaise longue,
while he played the gramophone,
record after record, walking without pause,
tracing the carpet's pattern with his feet.

Jazz, Debussy, jazz, Ravel, jazz,
Respighi, Stravinsky, jazz, Brahms. . . .

Then she said, " It is late. I must go. . . ."
He said, " I know."

He drew the curtains, closing the windows
to shut out the harsh amber moon,
the cloying insistence of orange-bloom,
the clamorous histrionics of three mocking-birds.

From the shadows of the corner
flowed Parsifal.

He knelt beside her shoulder,
and looked carefully at her closed eyes.

The ending, of course.
Always, forever after,
acquaintances, casually meeting,
chatting pleasantries.
Friends, without doubt,
strangers, certainly.

The music flowed.
Steadily he put forth his hand.
He drew his fingers, with a half-touch,
across the delicate eyelids,
down the joyous tilt of her nose,
brushing her lips,
along the soft chiseling of the cheeks and chin.

He dropped his hand to his side.
He would not forget.

The music faded.
Machinery clicked.
No sound.

Thus he knelt, and watched,
and the music streamed on within him,
and she lay in a pool of tenderness and peace.

And he knew that Beauty came through the velvet silence,
and smiled, and held her great, cool arms about them. . . .

So, for a dozen heart-beats.
Then silently she arose, and he arose,
and silently they rode through the throbbing night
to the single, quick, irrevocable word
" Good-by! " . . .

Don Juan set forth to conquer,
  all in his peacock pride.
He was debonair of glance,
  he was sure of stride.
He would have his way with any maid
  In all the countryside.

Conquest lost its savor
  ere it was scarce begun.
Words came scurrying through his brain,
  and he began to run:

" I want always to be a little boy,
  and have fun! "

Poor, confused, wee man —
Don Pan.

There was much pomposity and smugness
at the commencement of this recital
of ecstatic assets. Pride of possession
persuaded me of distinction. I was unique.
I thought, " À bas les Smiths et Browns et Joneses! "

Now, as I finger the spiritual savings,
I begin to perceive. . . .

Ah, Smith-Jones-Brown, will you bear with me a space?
May I boast of my-your treasures a little further?
I must begin to lump items, thus:
Section X, Unearned Ecstatic Income,
from sources such as the following:

Beethoven, Conrad, Raffael, Shelley, Bach,
Emily Dickinson, Michelangelo,
Puccini, Rimsky-Korsakov, Cézanne,
Hemingway, Shakespeare, Barrie, Debussy, Yeats,
Wagner, Millay, Charpentier, Rupert Brooke.
Browning, Keats, Stephens, Shaw, Virginia Woolf,
Da Vinci, Botticelli, Brahms, Ravel,
Rembrandt, Praxiteles and Richard Strauss —
acknowledgment is hereby gratefully made
of gifts, in rhythm of sound or line or word,
which quickened the pulsations of my heart,
and smoothed the crumpled edges of my soul.

And now . . . received from other sources,
remembered at random:
From a certain dozen persons
who knew me well — at my worst
if not at my best — some understanding,
much more forgiveness, and a stanch affection.

From dogs, three of them,
a fine, unreasoning faith,
gay comradeship, and blind, unswerved devotion.

From a woman, who had hated me,
one sentence, in after years:
" You are not my kin —
you have become more than kin."

From an old priest, in a tiny French village
called Laguiolle, one unforgettable hour
when he told, with a deep, firm simplicity
of how his life had attained its dreamed-of goal
in procuring farm-machinery for his peasants.

From a maiden, the honor of her confidence.
She bared the stumbling secrets,
ambitions, yearnings and visions
of a heart candid with rapturous integrity.

From a group of unknown punters, several minutes.
Of a sudden, they slid from a mist upon the Thames,
into the twinkling fairy lights of Bray,
on a June night, as we sat sipping Cointreau;
they were singing softly; they moved with a faint plash;
they slipped among the feathery willows, and vanished.

From an old white farmhouse, a quiet welcome;
it sat serene among the green of shrubs,
peering benignly through a haze of cherry-blossoms.

From my son, several moments; as when, for the first time,
he gravely walked and talked with me,
treating me as companion, not as parent . . .
and . . . on a hundred other small occasions. . . .

(Ah, do not fear. I shall not thrust upon you
bundles of charming domesticities,
the gentle, tedious, minor satisfactions
of hearth and field . . . nor shall I render praises
to mother, father, brother . . . there is no need.
No, Brown-Jones-Smith, we have known what we have
    known.)

The inventory limps into outright prose.
Let it close.

XIII

To you, who have given to me the priceless gift
of your love,
at whose mere name
my being glows with a life-giving flame,
who are, for me,
the sum and substance of all poetry,
what tribute adequately can I offer?

Shall I make a wish that you might share,
when we have shed these husks, a dreamless sleep,
beyond defeat, a grateful oblivion
throughout all time?
Or . . . may I proffer
deliberate understatement?
Attempt a whimsicality,
and, while emotions are surging strong as the sea,
Make ripples of preciosity?
Shall I make a jigging little rhyme,
a skittish scherzo? . . . so:

> Dear, I have an invitation to extend.
> Would you care to spend
> Eternity with me?
> Might I suggest
> that you shall be my guest
> at a small table, spread under a huge tree,

at an hour that will forever be
a little after three
of a sun-drenched day
in early May?

You shall sit there
endlessly at ease,
eternally young and fair
(if you shall so please)
and I will take care
to be a protean ghost,
shifting through the various me's
you have approved most,
according to your varying desire.

And we shall chat, and everything we say
shall be profound or witty, wise or gay.
And we will not tire.

At intervals shall appear —
as you shall wish —
an old waiter, fetching whatever dish
you have best enjoyed here,
and perhaps long drafts of golden Munich
      beer
in a cool, heavy stein,
or some light, joyous wine
of Bordeaux, or the Rhine.
Then, to our small table
under the huge tree
shall saunter, as we call,
those folk whom we

have loved, who have loved us.
And they shall share
our happiness. . . .
And all of us shall know
the answers to all questions.
Neither pain nor care
shall come to mar the timeless flow
of tranquillity. . . .

XIV

Ah, no.
This is tame quaintness.
It is unworthy.
I shall have, in a little space,
one final word for you.

Meanwhile,
I have completed my inventory,
such as it is,
surveyed my assets,
struck my trial balance.
It does not seem enough,
this that I have stored. . . .
It must serve.
Perhaps . . . for the lean years . . .
if I could purchase with it
a spiritual annuity . . .
so many ecstasies at what per cent? . . .

Shut the ledger. . . .

Now . . . the one word more.

When what of you that was you
and what of me that was I
shall be at last set free,

315

could we but be
vibrations of one note in one great chord,
forever unresolved,
sounding an ultimate ecstasy
into infinity!

E. & O. E.

THE TEXT OF THIS BOOK IS SET IN GRANJON, *a type named in compliment to* ROBERT GRANJON, *type-cutter and printer — Antwerp, Lyons, Rome, Paris — active from 1523 to 1590. The boldest and most original designer of his time, he was one of the first to practise the trade of type-founder apart from that of printer.*

This type face was designed by GEORGE W. JONES, *who based his drawings upon a type used by* CLAUDE GARAMOND *(1510–61) in his beautiful French books, and more closely resembles Garamond's own than do any of the various modern types that bear his name.*

This book was composed, printed, and bound by THE PLIMPTON PRESS, *Norwood, Mass. The paper was made by* S. D. WARREN CO., *Boston. The binding was designed by* W. A. DWIGGINS.